L.C. 3/12

DI000984

# Germany and Europe

# Germany and Europe

## Reflections on German Foreign Policy

Heinrich Von Brentano

*Translated from the German by* Edward Fitzgerald

*Foreword by* Chancellor Ludwig Erhard

*Acc. no. 78710*

FREDERICK A. PRAEGER, *Publisher*
NEW YORK

EDWARD MINER GALLAUDET MEMORIAL LIBRARY
GALLAUDET COLLEGE
WASHINGTON, D. C.

BOOKS THAT MATTER

Published in the United States of America in 1964
by Frederick A. Praeger, Inc., Publisher
111 Fourth Ave., New York 3, N.Y.

*All rights reserved*

© 1962 by Heinrich von Brentano

© This translation 1964 by André Deutsch Limited

Originally published under the title *Deutschland, Europa und die
Welt* by Siegler & Co. KG, Bonn – Wien – Zurich

Library of Congress Catalog Card Number: 64–23325

Printed in Great Britain

327.43
B38d Ef

# Foreword

Heinrich von Brentano was Germany's Foreign Minister for six years that were decisive for European and world politics. At a time when the great aims of the Atlantic Community and the prospect of consolidating Free Europe are in the foreground of discussion his speeches on foreign policy are of both historical and topical interest.

The subjects dealt with in the speeches contained in this book cover a wide field, from the economic amalgamation of the three Western zones of occupation in Germany to the creation of European Communities and the prospect opening up for the Atlantic Community. They represent the opinions of a responsible German statesman who has done much to bring his country back into the community of free peoples, to consolidate the association of the European countries which have signed the Treaty of Rome, and to strengthen NATO. These speeches will be of particular interest to the historian because they will allow him to study the motives and rationale of Germany's foreign policy in a decisive phase of European history. The economist will find that they confirm and justify the close interdependence of foreign policy and economics. For the politician they will serve as an example of a policy pursued from profound conviction.

For the reader who wishes to assess questions of international politics, an understanding of the German problem and post-war developments in Europe is particularly important. This book will help him to such an understanding.

LUDWIG ERHARD

Chancellor of the German Federal Republic

# Contents

*Contents*

8

# 1

# The German Länder and their Political Tasks*

THE unconditional surrender of May 1945 was the end of the long and painful false path the German people were forced to take under the sway of crime and irresponsibility. The ineffaceable traces of that false path were marked by streams of blood, widespread suffering, destruction and devastation; and along that path the German people lost everything that belongs integrally to the life of a civilized nation: justice, liberty, courage, pride, human dignity, and – not least – love. And with the logic immanent in the law of *horror vacui*, nature's abhorrence of a vacuum, the place of these lost qualities was filled with their opposites: lawlessness, slavery, cowardice, arrogance, presumption and hatred. Our people stood on the edge of a precipice, bewildered and confused, and abandoned by those who had claimed to be their leaders and demanded loyalty and obedience unto death. Our country was split up into fractions which owed their existence to geographical factors, temporary political and economic necessities, and the egocentric and egoistic interests and political or strategic considerations of the victorious powers. The constitutional structure of the Länder and the Reich was destroyed; the economy, as far as it had survived the war, was crippled. Chaos seemed victorious, and the people lived on in apathy and hopeless despair.

When we compare those conditions with the situation today we feel inclined to record great progress and give way to a certain optimism. Indeed, in retrospect it would be wrong and unjust to deny

*Speech delivered on January 7th 1947 on the governmental declaration made by Christian Stock (of the Social-Democratic Party) on January 6th 1947 on behalf of the newly-formed Hessian coalition government of the Social-Democratic Party and the Christian-Democratic Union, and on the final report of the retiring Minister-President, Professor Doctor Karl Geiler.

the progress which has been made and the successes which have been obtained with regard to our political development and consolidation, particularly in the three Länder of the American zone of occupation. Immediately after the complete collapse new political forces began to stir in the German people, forces which had been suppressed but which had never died altogether; and, with what was to hand, they now set out to achieve a re-shaping of political, economic and cultural life, to clear away the ruins, and to rebuild the basis of German national vitality, which had never been entirely destroyed. In those days we needed the unselfish and generous acceptance of responsibility by men who were willing and determined to rejoin the broken threads and to clear away the ruins with resolution but without destroying anything which could be preserved and was worth preserving, and so carry out the preliminary work essential for reconstruction.

Yesterday we heard the final report of Minister-President Professor Doctor Geiler, who has held the reins of government in our particular homeland, Hessen, since the autumn of 1945, and who is now handing them over to the first constitutionally elected Minister-President. We associate ourselves with the observations of Minister-President Stock, who began his governmental declaration by saying that it was his personal pleasure and parliamentary duty to express thanks to his retiring predecessor. The parliamentary Christian-Democratic Union party also takes this opportunity to thank Minister-President Professor Doctor Geiler and all those who were associated with him in whatever capacity, and to do so now on its behalf gives me particular satisfaction. Whoever looks back at the development in this period and considers the amount of valuable and constructive work that was done under the most unfavourable internal and external conditions cannot but express not only his sincere gratitude but also his honest admiration for what has been achieved. Let us not forget that the Land Hessen first came into being when the Cabinet was formed, and that thus from the very first day there was a tremendous amount of supplementary work to be done to gather districts together which had previously been administratively and politically separated.

The Länder Council was formed in this period in order to secure the closest possible political and economic co-ordination of the three Länder of the American zone, and to begin the bi-zonal negotiations between the American and the British zones and bring them to a successful conclusion. What was achieved in these respects was particularly in accord with the aims and desires of the retiring Minister-President, who was one of the first in Germany – and this deserves to be remembered again and again – to stress the necessity most urgently for us all to look beyond the borders of the Länder and the zones to our greater German homeland. It was he who worked untiringly and successfully to build bridges beyond the borders of the Länder and the zones; and – as we hope and trust – they will prove of lasting value on the way to German unity.

To pretend that a government which was formed out of nothing, which found itself daily faced with new and urgent tasks, which had to work under the most difficult political and economic conditions, whose composition not unnaturally involved internal strains, and which was forced under the pressure of circumstances to exercise both legislative and executive power – to pretend that such a government was without fault would be less than honest; indeed it would rob our thanks of credibility and deprive them of real value.

We consider it particularly necessary to say this because in doing so we are expressing the earnest desire not only of our own parliamentary party but surely of the whole Landtag, so that the new Cabinet may never forget for any reason, no matter how honestly conceived, that a clear and definite separation between the executive and the legislative is an essential condition for the development of true democracy.

My party will always uphold and defend the rights of the people's representation – not in order to cramp the enthusiasm of the Cabinet in its work, but to ensure that the principles of our new political life as laid down in the constitution may be unswervingly upheld.

There was tremendous political development in Hessen during the term of office of the retiring Minister-President. The formation of political parties was followed by the municipal elections. The preparatory constitutional commission and the advisory Land committee were convened, the constitutional advisory Land assembly was elected, and the elections to the first Landtag took place together with the voting on the new constitution of Hessen. Yesterday, before this Landtag, Minister-President Stock presented the first Cabinet formed on a parliamentary basis.

The government declaration to which we listened yesterday expressed the earnestness with which the Cabinet proposes to deal with the problems facing us; and this is a very good thing indeed, because although we have good reason to congratulate ourselves on the progress we have made in our inner-political development, it would be irresponsible self-deception to attempt to conceal the great seriousness of the situation. In his first speech on December 20th 1946 Minister-President Stock declared: 'In serving Hesse we serve the German people.' We concur wholeheartedly. If the developments of the past few months have produced anything of value it is this above all: it has extended our vision for the great aims and tasks of the present time, and it has given us the right, and also imposed on us the duty, to make it very clear here in the Landtag of Hesse that we are thinking with profound concern of the fate and the future of our greater German homeland. Speaking on February 26th 1941, the chairman of my parliamentary party, my friend Doctor Köhler, who has been prevented by a serious accident from being here today and expressing the views of my party, declared at the opening of the advisory Land committee: 'The principle laid down by the Potsdam conference, that the economic unity of Germany should be preserved, represents a decisive credit item in our total political balance sheet. It forms the fundamental basis for the reconstruction of Germany's economy and thus for the freedom of our people to develop.'

I repeat these observations here in order to indicate that they have lost nothing of their importance in the meantime, but also in order to raise the question, dictated by profound anxiety, of what has been done in the meantime to carry out the principle proposed then. We are firmly convinced that Germany's fate is indissolubly bound up with the fate of Europe, and the fate of Europe with that of the world. Whoever expresses any doubt on this point would merely show that he had learned nothing from the historical events of recent years.

Germany must be administered as an economic unit. The zonal borders must completely disappear. Economic rapprochement is essential not only for Germany's future but for that of Europe as well. In many economic questions Germany is not governed by the Control Commission, but nor does this body permit her to govern herself. Millions of Germans must not be forced to live in uncertainty as to their fate. No one has the right to deprive the German people of the opportunity to work their own way out of their troubles and difficulties so long as they respect human liberty and do not deviate from the path of peace. Germany should not be held vassal to any power or group of powers; she should not be treated as a pawn in a game of power-politics. Germany must once again have a government and be given an opportunity to work her way back to an honourable place amongst the peace-loving nations of the world.

These remarks have been taken literally from a speech delivered by the American Secretary of State for Foreign Affairs, Mr Byrne, in Stuttgart on September 8th 1946. I will not conceal the accompanying observations to the effect that Germany must recognize the reasons for her own difficulties and learn from them. We do not fail to recognize the truth of this, but there is something else which is also very clear to us: a people whose thoughts and actions, plans and projects are overshadowed by day to day anxieties that are increasing to an alarming extent, which suffers from hunger and cold, which has no proper roof over its head, and which lives in constant fear of unemployment, can easily fall victim to nihilistic despair and complete disaster. Distress, worry and anxieties are not a favourable basis for building up a new democracy. No new political conception can take root in such soil. We therefore support the appeal of the Minister-President to world public opinion, and insist that the German people have a right to live, and that anyone who seeks to deprive them of this right offends against the spirit of mankind.

We deputies, who possess the mandate of our constituents, who have received from them the task of building up a new democratic State, and of shouldering and ameliorating their burdens, will regard it as our solemn task to carry out the principles laid down in the constitution and to translate the contents of that constitution from the sphere of abstract thought to that of practical politics. We must raise our voices in the knowledge that time is short. It is our solemn task to see to it that the German people are not treated as a passive object of world events, and that they are not used as a pawn in power-political wranglings, but are given an opportunity of presenting their own problems. Only by the increased responsibility that this involves – a responsibility that may sometimes appear almost unbearable to us – will it be possible to create conditions in which the German people can be brought to recognize the profound seriousness of their situation and at the same time be given the assurance that with the support of the victorious powers they will be able to build up a new life for themselves in peaceable and industrious labour. We in the Christian-Democratic Union firmly believe that inner moral renewal is an essential condition for the general recuperation of the German people. A new German State can arise only if it has the support of morally renewed men and women who are prepared to advance

13

beyond the limits laid down by knowledge into the sphere of absolute values; because there and there alone lie the never-failing sources of understanding, the essential and inviolable basis of human existence and human development. We are firmly convinced that the strength and courage to build up a new Germany and to lead our Fatherland out of these chaotic conditions can be found only in the Christian ethic and in the spiritual tradition of Western Christian civilization. We further believe that Rationalism is no more able than Materialism to solve the great problems of our day. Perhaps in times of political and economic normality man's mind and man's reason alone may be sufficient, but in times of extreme tribulation only the heart can count. When limits are imposed from without on State sovereignty, and thus on our own demands and desires, it is only man's feelings and aspirations that can exceed those limits without creating resentment and leading to misunderstanding.

At this hour we join with the government declaration in expressing the wish that the millions of German prisoners of war may soon be sent back to their homes, particularly as so many of them have been living for so long in bitter moral and material affliction. We believe that we are entitled to keep on putting this demand forward, since even where written standards of justice are absent there are still inherent conceptions of justice, whether they are based on the Christian ethic or on generally valid moral ideas concerning the peaceful relations of nations.

We also have in mind the fate of millions of fugitives, who not only lost all their possessions in total warfare like many millions of other Germans, but who also through no fault of their own lost their homeland as well. We are anxious to help them, and we will help them, but we cannot conceal the fact that over-populated West Germany will not be able to receive them and offer them the basis on which to build up a new existence. Germany will never be viable within her present frontiers, and deprived of her material basis she will never be able to recognize those frontiers, since they have been drawn arbitrarily and by force, and not by law and justice, and – what is much more – she could not do so without risking her national dignity: something which even a defeated people should not be denied.

With deep satisfaction we learn that in deciding such questions the victorious countries are not prepared to recognize merely the normative force of existing facts as a definitive solution. However, recently, and in particular now, before the opening of peace negotiations, voices have also been heard pretending that the present situation and the present frontiers are in accordance with the wishes of the populations concerned. This has been said of the frontiers both in the West and in the East. But when we consider the West and the East we must say that such suggestions are untrue. As a result of the fortunes of war large parts of the population of Germany's eastern provinces were evacuated to remoter areas. Later on warlike operations extended to these areas too, and finally complete collapse came about. In the meantime we have learnt of the agreements of the Great Powers in the Atlantic Charter, the decisions arrived at in Yalta, and those come to in Potsdam. These decisions involved strategic war aims. But we cannot grant such agreements the status of international law and justice. Something like ten million people have been compelled, most of them by force, to leave their home territories, where for centuries without interruption they tilled the soil and kept the economy in being. In so doing they made their peaceable contribution to the flourishing development of Europe. These men and women now hope, and will continue to hope, that natural law and the rights of man will be recognized in any frontier settlement; that Germany's eastern territories will be returned to her, and that they will once again be placed under German administration. As justified as the strategic aims embodied in the decisions of Yalta and the Atlantic Charter may have been, they do not represent a suitable basis for a constructive peace. The Yalta and Potsdam conferences adopted the aims of war, not those of peace. These conferences did not prepare the way for a lasting peace.

The peace negotiations will also have to deal with the question of reparations. These too must presuppose the viability of the German people. But this viability – as we can see more clearly every day – is most seriously endangered. The danger comes in equal measure from the material dismantling, the dismantling of whole industrial undertakings, and from the dismantling of personnel – and this is a very serious matter. Skilled workmen and scientists whose services are essential for Germany's reconstruction are being taken away.

When we talk of reparations there is one thing we should like to make very clear: let no one anywhere believe that there are Germans worthy of the name who, in order to reduce their own share of the post-war burdens, would be prepared for one moment to consider ceding the homeland of their German fellow citizens in payment.

15

We would sooner take on greater burdens and carry them for a longer time than betray our own people.

We are also in agreement with the governmental declaration that the restoration of Germany's economic and political unity is the preliminary condition for her economic and political reconstruction.

We regard the Länder Council and the bi-zonal institutions as a necessary transitional solution, but as long as these emergency make-shifts exist we demand that they should be democratically re-shaped and that they should not continue to work, as they have done so far, bureaucratically – even autocratically.

We have heard the declaration of the government with satisfaction, because in this point too the political aims of the Cabinet accord with our own.

In particular we underline the statement of the government that we must acknowledge the State based on law as the basis on which free men must live together, and that the concept of law must imbue our whole public and private life. We therefore welcome the plans and the intentions of the Cabinet. Although we repeat that the liberation of the German people from the spirit of nationalism and militarism is the unquestionable preliminary condition for the development of a new democracy we cannot overlook the fact that the application of the law of March 5th 1946* has resulted in a political crisis whose importance can hardly be over-estimated. It is not surprising that a law without precedent in legal history should reveal defects in application, particularly since it seeks to amalgamate German and foreign legal concepts in a way which is not, in my opinion, very successful. But over and above this, the way in which the law has been applied has grossly accentuated these defects. Therefore on this point in particular there is need for a carefully considered but speedy and thorough reform. The aim of such a reform will not be to save convicted evil-doers, the henchmen of the National-Socialist terrorist régime, from the hands of justice, but to place justice in the place of arbitrariness, to introduce uniformity in place of diversity, and the spirit of reconciliation instead of the spirit of vengeance. It seems to me of particular importance that any political abuse of this law should be excluded once and for all. Even those against whom this law operates must be given the feeling that justice has once again become the basis of the new democracy.

*This law for freedom from National Socialism and militarism applied to the American zone.

The question of reparations, which was also touched on by the Minister-President, is directly connected with the application of this law, whose aims we also accept. We are not dealing here with considerations which might perhaps be dictated by political expedience, but with moral obligations which the whole German people must freely recognize and take upon themselves. The degree of willingness with which this duty is carried out will be a yardstick for the German people and for the whole world to measure the depth of our new-won understanding.

The parliamentary Christian-Democratic Union party will pay particular attention to the re-shaping of our cultural life. We feel that in this respect the very basis itself is in need of renewal. The Christian tradition must once again take its proper place in public and private life, in our schools, high schools and universities, and we are firmly convinced that without this there can never be any successful moral renewal of the German people.

In answer to the representative of the Liberal-Democratic Party who deplored the absence in the government declaration of any reference to a planned and guided cultural policy I should like to say: in this respect we are not in favour of State planning, and it is no business of the State to pursue a cultural policy; the only task of the State is to create the conditions in which cultural projects can develop.

A further very essential and urgent task of the Cabinet and of parliament will be to carry out the principles of the constitution in the economic and social sphere – not merely to the letter, but also in the spirit and meaning of the constitution. To those who doubt this intention I can reply: the constitution came into being as a result of co-operation between the two coalition parties, and therefore these two parties are best fitted to put the constitution into operation.

The Christian-Democratic Union, which took an influential and decisive part in the drafting of the constitution, was attacked just now by our colleague Herr Bauer, who declared that his party had been taken by surprise by the constitutional compromise arrived at between the Christian-Democratic Union and the Social-Democratic Party, but was resolved not to be taken by surprise again. The Christian-Democratic Union will take an equally influential and decisive part in carrying out the constitution.

We are also anxious that the present controlled economy, which is disagreeable in every respect and was the result of the exceptionally difficult times, should be replaced as soon as possible by a sensible free economy which will seek to provide our needs without excluding or hampering the creative free enterprise of the individual.

We are also well aware that the solution of both our political and our economic problems will depend to a great extent on the support we receive from the military government.

The food situation is serious, even critical. The fuel shortage affects not only individuals, but also our economy; and this is even more serious, since the coal shortage and the direct or indirect interruptions in the power supply threaten us with complete economic collapse. The raw-material basis of our industry has shrunk to a minimum because the low stocks we had at the time of our defeat have in the meantime been exhausted. Before long we shall not be in a position to produce even the most urgently needed consumer goods. We are approaching the victorious powers for raw-material credits precisely because we do not wish to beg for alms. We are grateful to the military government for the support we have received in the transitional period. We now want to revive our industry, and in particular our manufacturing industry, in order that we may be in a position to buy on the free market those things we require to meet our needs.

It would take too long to deal with all the tasks which will face the Landtag and the Cabinet in the near future. We feel that we are in a position to approve the government declaration, and we are particularly glad that the Cabinet has made no promises it will be unable to fulfil.

Many difficult tasks lie ahead of us, and we shall be able to perform them only if parliament and the Cabinet work together in harmony, and if our people are ready and determined to make even the greatest sacrifices. But this places an obligation on parliament and on the Cabinet to practise the utmost economy not only in expenditure but also in the application of new resources. If we are to create the conditions for healthy economic reconstruction then we must emerge from the state of political uncertainty in which we have been living up to now and enter into a phase of political stability.

# 2

# The Problem of De-nazification*

A VERY great deal has already been said about the problem of de-nazification, both with regard to general principles and to its particular aspects. I think it is not too much to say that most people feel that in the year during which the law has been in operation defects have been revealed not only in the law itself, but also in its execution. When we now criticize both the law and its execution I should like to preface my remarks with one observation on the origin of the law itself; it was not adopted by the German people in the ordinary way, but was drawn up in co-operation with the representatives of the Military Government; it was placed on the Statute Book without the authority of parliament, which did not exist at the time; and it was signed, as we all know, very reluctantly by the Prime Ministers of the three Länder of the American Zone, and only because they felt that almost any sacrifice was worth while in order to take the process of de-nazification out of the hands of the occupation authorities and place it in German hands.

We are aware that we are not in a position to make any changes in this law, which was issued on a Länder Council basis, and that when we desire to criticize this law we must confine ourselves to requesting the Government to put forward our proposals to the Military Government through the appropriate channels.

As far as the process of de-nazification itself is concerned, it lies largely in German hands, and therefore to a certain limited extent

---

*Speech delivered on July 4th 1947 following a statement by the Hessian Minister for Political Liberation, Gottlieb Binder (SPD), on the problem of de-nazification.

we are in a position to exercise influence on its administration. I am prefacing my observations in this way because I am anxious to make it quite clear, and clear in particular to the Minister for Political Liberation himself, that we have no intention of reproaching the Government with matters for which it bears no responsibility. We must all realize that the Government has had to follow a prearranged course. We should also like to express our appreciation of the fact that as far as possible the Government has done its best to take into account the objections which have been raised; and that – once again as far as possible – it has sought to influence the occupation authorities to change the law itself and the manner of its execution. I therefore strongly disagree with the member of this House who declared here that the whole administration of the law in the American Zone or in Hesse has been nothing less than a fiasco.

For my part I feel that such irresponsible generalizations contribute nothing whatever to our efforts to come to grips with a very serious problem. I also think it just as wrong and senseless to pick out individual examples which no one here is in a position to check, and then use them as a basis for claiming that the law itself is bad and the work of the courts defective. When we are told that a certain industrialist – call him what you like – possesses a fortune of two and a half million marks, and yet this man has been grouped with those minor offenders who have got away with a fine of 2,000 marks, then I am quite unimpressed with the logic of the argument, because how much a man possesses is nothing to do with his offence. The maximum fine of 2,000 marks was fixed by the Military Government. I do not think, and I never did think, that this was a particularly good solution of the problem, because it involves a uniformity of which I certainly do not approve, since I am in favour of considering the individual circumstances and the individual offender.

One more thing must be said here and now quite frankly, and that is that we are still faced with a serious crisis in the process of denazification and that I can see no signs of any improvement. In this respect I am unable to share even the relative optimism of the Minister. According to his statement, with the present regulations and the present procedure it is likely to take between four and five years before the backlog of cases can be dealt with, and this fills us with dismay. It means that it will take something like five years before the last proceedings under the law of March 5th 1946 will be concluded, not counting the possibility of appeal procedure. But the fact is that unless we can find some way of co-operating with the Military Government so that the procedure is speeded up to secure a settlement of all our outstanding de-nazification problems by next summer, the reconstruction of our country will be endangered.

What is really and truly the nature of the crisis? I have the impression that public discussion is paying too much attention to symptoms, and that we lack either the understanding or the courage to go to the root of the matter. Now when this law was first promulgated General Clay made a statement which, with the permission of the Speaker, I propose to repeat here. It strikes me as important that we should remember it ourselves and that we should remind the Military Government that it has not yet been complied with. General Clay declared that it was the avowed and constantly maintained policy of the U.S. Military Government to transfer the administration and the government in the American Zone to German hands as soon as possible. This involved rights, but also duties and responsibilities, and he was well aware of the sincerity and the conscientiousness with which the Prime Ministers had tackled the new laws. But as good, as healthy and as reasonable as a law might be, it needed the confidence of the majority of the people before it could be properly administered.

I think it is not too much to say that the majority of our people no longer have confidence in this law, and that therefore the assumptions on which it was promulgated no longer exist. It does not surprise me in the least that we are forced to this conclusion, because in promulgating it the legislature ventured into virgin territory. A law which seeks to lay down responsibility for a past epoch is without precedent in the history of jurisprudence. And when such a law is nevertheless passed as the result of co-operation between people who, whilst pursuing the same ultimate objectives, proceed from totally different assumptions, and when it comes into being as a compromise between German and Anglo-Saxon ideas of jurisprudence, then such a law inevitably carries within itself the seeds of just such a false development as we are compelled to recognize frankly today.

Doctor Fritzle, an official of the Stuttgart administration, has dealt with this law in a study which strikes me as important. She writes:

'In so far as the Liberation Law proposes to make up for a German revolution which did not come about it misses its objective – quite apart from the fact that a revolution cannot be

21

carried out by law or by anything remotely resembling legal procedure. A revolution must necessarily take place outside any ordinary forms of legal procedure, but it must nevertheless aim at the establishment of a legal order.'

In another passage she writes:

'The promulgation of a law to carry out a political purge has removed the matter into the sphere of jurisprudence, but this then involves an obligation to respect the forms and restrictions of normal legal procedure. Any reluctance to comply with this obligation involves only too readily a danger that the law will be abused. The administration of a law involves the use of force, but whoever uses force without respecting the restrictions of the law is behaving – whatever the differences of degree – as Hitler and his accomplices behaved.'

She is right in saying that to invoke legislation involves the acceptance of certain restrictions, including an obligation to remain within legal bounds. I feel that the administration of this law has been unsatisfactory in so many cases precisely because it offends that respect for law felt, I am sure I am right in saying, by the majority of the German people.

This morning Doctor Becker pointed out that there may well have been National Socialists who, though active, were not guilty in any criminal sense. This aroused disagreement from various others here, but I do not hesitate to say that in principle I agree with him. When we are dealing with the question of guilt we must first make up our minds exactly what guilt is. Unfortunately the law omits to do just this. I am sure you are all familiar with the extremely interesting and important essay in which Professor Jaspers of Heidelberg deals with the question of guilt. He draws a distinction between various kinds of guilt, and he shows most convincingly that there was political guilt, and that as a collective we cannot shake off our responsibility for it. He then goes on to point out that in addition to this political guilt there was also moral guilt, the moral guilt of those who against their inner conviction and against their better knowledge supported a movement and a cause which they recognized, or should have recognized, as bad. In addition, he says, there is a third form of guilt, criminal guilt; the sort of guilt that falls within the penal code. Finally there is a fourth kind of guilt, metaphysical guilt;

the kind of guilt that in one way or another we must all acknowledge for the whole deplorable development that took place from
1933 to 1945.

Writing on the recovery of the German people, Professor Barth has
declared:

> 'What we must do now, all of us, every group, stratum, class,
> party or tendency in the German people, is to ask ourselves what
> was the special error which caused us and our friends, and those
> who thought like us, to contribute to the catastrophe which, in
> effect, all of us together brought about, and under which all of us
> together are now suffering. We ourselves, not someone else, we
> with our wisdom or folly, selfishness or frivolity, made possible the
> great miscalculation from 1933 to 1945.'

I think it would be a good thing if when the German people start
to examine their past – which is necessary and should be carried out
without feelings of hatred, but with all possible trenchancy – they
should first ask themselves this question. Nothing would be worse
than to let ourselves be manoeuvred into a Pharisaical attitude in
facing this important political and moral problem. We must not only
ask to what extent others were guilty, we must also ask what guilt
we bear ourselves. More than one false note was sounded in today's
discussion. It is only too easy to blame someone else – at the same
time indirectly proclaiming one's own innocence.

In my opinion this question of guilt is cardinal in the administration of this law. We must not cease to oppose the completely false
and intrinsically evil principle which this law introduces: the imputa-
tion of guilt to large numbers of people unless they can prove that
during the twelve years in question they did nothing wrong. Why,
even with the most brutal of murderers we insist that the authorities
should not merely put him on trial, but that they should effectively
prove his guilt.

I am well aware that this comparison is not altogether valid, since
we are dealing here with a political question, but at the same time
it does serve to illustrate what I find fundamentally wrong with the
whole procedure. The sort of proof the law calls for under Appendix
A suffers from all the disadvantages of a questionnaire. Various
speakers here have pointed out – and I agree with them – that such
methods tend to catch the man whose answers to the questionnaire
give rise to suspicion, whilst missing the man whose answers are

23

satisfactory even though there are crimes on his conscience. Now when we call for a change in the law we are doing, in fact, no more than suggesting that an Order of the Control Commission itself should be carried out. I am referring to Directive No. 38 of the Allied Control Commission for all occupation zones in Germany. This directive embodies the de-nazification law, but at the same time it contains an important provision, namely that zonal commanders may issue special instructions within its general framework.

Otherwise the law as embodied in directive No. 38 is in much the same form as we have it, but with the difference that it talks frankly of punishment and not of atonement – and this, in my view, is all to the good. Referring to those whose responsibility was primary, and to the activists who come under Appendix A, it also contains this provision:

> 'If the results of the investigation make legal proceedings necessary, those concerned must be put on trial as primarily responsible, and, if found guilty, punished.'

In other words, the Allied Control Commission also proceeds on the assumption that such cases should be dealt with as cases are everywhere else in the civilized world; namely, that where there is a suspicion of guilt under Appendix A, the case must be properly proved.

It may perhaps be objected that the matter isn't so very important, but I disagree. On the contrary, I think it is a fundamental point – and particularly so when one thinks of Darmstadt camp. It is, God knows, a very unsatisfactory state of affairs – and we shall surely all be in agreement on this point – that thousands of people have been held for years now solely because of suspicion under Appendix A of the law of March 5th 1946. I do not want to take up your time by citing individual cases, but I must mention one: there was a young man in camp – he was released a week ago – whose only offence was that in 1933, when he was just nineteen years old, he joined the SA. Within six months he had realized that he was not in congenial company, and so he left the organization. From that time on – and the facts are not in dispute at all – he was a convinced opponent of the National Socialist movement. During the war this young man was called up and he served in the Army Administration Department. In the autumn of 1944 he was transferred to the Königsberg military district where he was informed that he was being seconded to the

Waffen-SS in his previous capacity. Because his job involved his holding rank he was then given his equivalent rank in the Waffen-SS, that of SS-Untersturmführer; certainly not a very exalted one. In the Waffen-SS he now did exactly what he had done before in the Army – probably working out the pay and allowances, or something of the sort. And because he had been compelled to serve, willy-nilly, for about three months in the Waffen-SS this young man had to spend two years in Darmstadt camp after the war.

I feel that this one example should be enough to convince everyone that any form of automatic procedure is false and senseless.

A good deal remains to be said about the law itself, but I think I shall meet with general approval if I confine my remarks to what is really essential, particularly as so much has already been said on the point. A few words on procedure, therefore. We have very good reason – and this goes for my Party too – to reject as wrong and unfair any attempt to condemn the whole activity of the courts in this question. On the contrary, we should appreciate that many honourable and responsible people have been found to take over a far from agreeable task and to carry it out purely from a sense of duty, and that they have done their best to act decently and correctly within the meaning of the law and in a spirit not only of liberation but also of reconciliation. In short, the behaviour of the majority of those concerned with the activities of these courts is worthy of our appreciation. We have no desire to include such people in our criticisms – in fact we should be only too glad that although they often find themselves in conflict with their own consciences they continue to do their jobs. I am convinced that the situation with regard to these courts is much the same as it is in any other part of the administrative apparatus. You hear nothing about a hundred honest bus conductors, whereas the man who steals fare money comes before the courts and, of course, into the newspapers. In the same way, no one here has mentioned the hundred and one unexceptionable verdicts, but individual verdicts which have seemed exceptionable have been picked out and criticized – very often without any attempt to go through the files first and find out something about the background.

The legal profession also came under fire here today. Now– perhaps for my sins – I belong to that profession, and at least I can claim that it teaches us to be cautious in our criticism. We know how easy it is to damn a judgement out of hand, and how difficult it is to sustain such a criticism. I therefore propose to confine my attacks to the defects of the system and of the court procedure as such. If we are honest we must admit that it was not easy to set up these courts at all, and I think we all agree that their composition – a chairman and four party representatives as jurors – is far from ideal. Of course, their task is a political one, and therefore it was probably not only right but even essential to enlist the political parties in this way. At the same time, this party-political complexion of the courts was bound now and again to lead to failures – not to use a more forceful term. And again if we are honest we shall also have to admit that the system has often been misused by political parties and their officials for purposes which have very little in common with those of the law as such – let me hasten to add that I am accusing no one in this matter. But the fact remains that the law has been used in this devious way to settle accounts with political and personal enemies. And it is still being so used. And when a judge or a prosecutor is not prepared to lend himself to such things he is dealt with too. No one can pretend that this is a satisfactory state of affairs, or that these matters have always been dealt with as they should have been by right. And here I am definitely criticizing the Liberation Ministry. I consider it intolerable that chairmen, or jurors, or prosecutors should be removed without a word of explanation to public opinion as to the reasons for their removal. We owe them this at least, since otherwise, unless the cause of their removal is made public, people are inclined to think that they must have done something dishonourable. The integrity of public life is best served by dealing openly with every known case of corruption, whether political, moral or material. I have deliberately referred to cases of corruption because although unfortunately they are by no means rare it is rarely that they come to the direct knowledge of the Ministry.

The problem of the investigators has also been touched on. The fact is that some of the people who have obtained such employment are not primarily interested in justice, and it is no accident that this kind of investigator takes up his inquiries with particular celerity and pursues them with particular zeal when the party concerned happens to possess, say, a prosperous farm. It is understandable perhaps, though not excusable, if the man's relatives then react to the more or less silly questions of the investigator by greasing his palm. But when the investigator himself demands a bribe, this is neither understandable nor tolerable, and he should be appropriately punished.

As we are discussing the question of corruption, we should not overlook the corruption amongst the accused themselves – even if the idea astonishes you. It is a fact that in many cases men are expected to denounce everything they previously upheld, and to uphold everything they previously denounced. This is not the right way to go about things, and it is a defect both of the law itself and of its administration. A man who joined the National Socialist Party in 1933 out of deep conviction should not be reproached with that now. I entirely agree with colleague Friedhof when he says that in 1931, 1932 and 1933 there were undoubtedly many people who did not realize how criminal the aims of the Nazi Party were, and who joined it, perhaps because they were politically simple-minded, because they were carried away, or because they were misled. These people are not to be put into the same class as those who voluntarily joined that band of criminals in the years 1938 to 1944 when everybody could see for himself just what was happening.

When we complain of procedural excesses then we must go further and see to it that something is done to regularize matters, and to this end the Ministry was asked a year ago to issue clear and unambiguous rules of procedure. The excesses complained of are still taking place and it is regrettable that the Ministry has so far done nothing to comply with that request, because cases of such importance require a procedure no less clear and established than that in any ordinary criminal case. The existing defects cannot be made good by merely issuing circulars, particularly when, far from supplementing, they sometimes contradict each other.

We have already made it quite clear that while we want the law administered in accordance with its spirit and purpose, we also require a number of amendments. This is the reason for the proposal my Party is placing before you today, in which it asks the Government to open negotiations with the Military Government with a view to securing certain changes in the law of March 5th 1946. This refers first of all to Article 40, because we hold that the severe measures it provides for, including arrest and sequestration, are not tolerable, even at the order of the chairman of the court, unless at the same time lawful means of appeal exist. In a State based on the rule of law such great powers should not be placed in the hands of an individual unless there is at the same time some control over him. Why, the Constitution itself provides that every arrest shall be examined by a judge! We are therefore anxious that the Liberation

Law should also contain a provision allowing appeal proceedings against measures taken by the chairmen of the courts.

In our opinion one of the most important of the many injustices the law has brought with it comes from the automatic obligation it contains according to which all those who are placed in Group III must show a minimum of two years good conduct. But there are many thousands who have been out of their jobs for at least two years, particularly minor officials who stood the full brunt of Nazi oppression and were least in a position to resist. Today they have already been unemployed and without earned income for two years, and in these two years they have already atoned more than someone who is, say, a member of a free profession and has had to deposit 2,000 marks as a Nazi camp follower. The time has come to be fair to these other people in two ways: first of all according to the joint resolution that the employment provision, which has already fulfilled its purpose, should now be withdrawn; and secondly by leaving it to the discretion of the court to fix the length of the probation period, and in doing so to take account of the period during which the person concerned has already been unemployed.

We also feel that the general provision that a person thus bound over should not be allowed to practice his profession should be qualified. You already know that in many small workshops employing less than ten people, or on farms, men are allowed to work even during the probationary period, whereas people engaged in the free professions, for example, doctors, are not allowed to practice their professions during this two-year period.

We also feel that it is high time to adapt the Liberation Law to Directive No. 38 of the Control Commission, dismiss the assumption of guilt, and re-establish the principle which prevails in all jurisprudence that the guilt of the individual must first be proved.

The United States Military Occupation Government has also issued instructions that interned people who belong to other zones can neither be brought before the courts, nor released as persons not belonging to groups affected by the Nuremberg judgement. We feel that this is excessively harsh and intolerable, and that there is no good reason why a person who cannot, or will not, return to the Eastern Zone should be kept indefinitely in a camp merely because he cannot be de-nazified at home. Logically it would mean that these people will have to spend the rest of their lives in a camp. We feel that arrangements should be made to bring them before the camp courts; and if this is done it will always be possible to conduct the investigations with special thoroughness.

We also feel that cases of automatic arrest should be checked as quickly as possible, because from every point of view it is a bad thing that 10,000 people should still be in Darmstadt camp when we know from the previous practice of the courts that at least four-fifths of them will not be sent to a labour camp. We therefore propose that this checking should be speeded up, and that the prosecutor shall have the right to call for the release of the person concerned and the transfer of the file to his home court in all cases where it appears unlikely that he would be sentenced to a term in a labour camp.

My time is running short, but in conclusion I will repeat that our intention to co-operate in the administration of the law is unchanged, but we do require that in every case the individual responsibility of the person concerned should be inquired into, that he should then be called to account according to the extent of his guilt, and that he should be tried according to normal legal procedure. At the same time I feel that the Ministry at least should use the possibility of quashing a judgement only in exceptional cases, and that it should not, for example, quash judgements which the Americans have already confirmed. Formalism can be pushed too far.

# 3

# The Bonn Statute*

AFTER all that has been said here it is not easy to find anything fundamentally new to say about the law which we now propose to give a third reading, particularly as time is getting short. However, I feel that it would be wrong to let the occasion pass without clarifying the political significance of what we are adopting. Today is May 8th, so that it is four years now since total war ended in total defeat. Today we have met here in Bonn to discuss the basis of a new and better State. In 1945 the German people were suffering from the shock of collapse. At that time there were no new political ideas, and for a variety of reasons it was impossible for us to come to grips in our minds with our immediate past. In the years that followed when the German people gradually recovered from the shock of the collapse they suffered more than one set-back and more than one disappointment. In those years we had to wrestle with the problem of whether it was possible at all to establish an organically developed democracy under the government of an occupying power. I think the doubts that arose were justified, and they still exist today. We must make up our minds about these doubts and realize the limits laid down for us by the facts of the case in order that we may be able to arrive at a proper understanding of what we must now do.

It has already been repeatedly pointed out that the sovereignty of the German people was never at any time extinguished. This is not only our political conviction, but it is also the legal view that has prevailed, since it was affirmed in a decision of the American

*Address to the Parliamentary Council on May 8th 1949, on the day that the Statute founding the German Federal Republic was adopted by 53 against 12 votes.

Supreme Court in June 1947. In the same way our right as Germans to re-order our State was also never curtailed. We must therefore dismiss the false suggestion that what we are now doing is being done by the right or permission of any third party. The right of Germans to re-order their German Fatherland on their own could never be abrogated because it is based directly on the duty of every German towards his own people. The authorization for us to implement this right could, however, be suspended by the victor. This authorization was given last summer. Now, although we should clearly realize the limits of our powers, nevertheless when we recall the years through which we have passed we have every reason to be satisfied with a political development in the western Zones during the past four years that in May 1945 even an optimist would have dismissed as utterly impossible.

At the same time our feeling of satisfaction at being in a position to tackle our own German tasks on our own responsibility, even if our independence is to some extent still limited, is mingled with deep sorrow that only a section of the German people is able to be represented here today to join with us in laying the basis of our new State. I have nothing to add to the regret that has already been expressed here. At the same time we are all quite clear on one point – and it is expressed in the final article of our draft constitution – namely, that what we are deciding here today can and must be only temporary. And we hope and trust that the day will soon come when what we are about to do will be out of date, and the whole German people will be freely in a position to decide the form of their own State and the elements of their own constitution.

Today we are about to take the first step in this process of becoming a State by adopting the constitution in its third reading. We are well aware that some of the members of this House will not vote for it, and this, I must point out, will include some of our closest friends. We have no desire to reproach them because we know that they will be acting according to their consciences, and that even after this decision we shall be one with them in our joint work on behalf of our German Fatherland. We know that if they feel now that they cannot go with us along the path we have chosen this will never separate us in our joint objective.

What there is to say about the constitution itself has already been said here by previous speakers, including the fact that no one in this House entirely approves of it. This is usually the case with laws of such fundamental importance. Compromises are part and parcel of political life. Those who reject compromises because they reject democracy as such are inclined to describe them falsely as horse-trading. It is certainly true that compromises must never be allowed to cross the borderline where matters of principle begin. I feel that we have, in fact, succeeded in keeping on the right side of this borderline, and that this is particularly true of my own party.

Ratification will be the second step we have to take. By a majority vote this House has already decided to leave the ratification to the Länder. Beyond saying that I regret it I do not want to criticize a decision that has already been made. Our colleague Heuss has spoken very cogently on what our attitude to the Constitution should be, and how we can best secure integration. Personally I feel that the best thing would have been to let the people themselves decide.

The elections will now follow, and those elected, and all the organs of the new Federation: the Federal President, the Federal Government, the Federal Council and the Federal Landtag – right down to the elector himself – will have to inform this law with living spirit, to bring dead words to life. The conditions under which we have to live will not make this easy. At this juncture I should like to appeal to the occupying powers to exercise the occupation statute, under which we shall presumably still have to live for a while (until it is replaced by a peace treaty to which, I feel, we are already entitled), in the spirit of its preamble and in particular in the spirit of its accompanying text. If this is done then this statute, of which no German can wholly approve, will at least not hinder us in our efforts to build up a democracy stemming from our people and understood by them.

The way will then be open for us – and here I take the opportunity to welcome a fundamental change in the outlook of the Allies – to co-operate in a really united Europe, a co-operation based on equal rights, such as was first mentioned in the letter of the Foreign Ministers of April 22nd. This will then allow us to make that great contribution to the world that the American Secretary of State Dean Acheson hoped of us in his speech of April 28th.

But here, too, just one word of qualification; namely, that we hope and trust that the occupation powers will be conscious of the duties which are corollary to the rights they have assumed over us.

In conclusion I should like to recall something I read in a book

4

## German

iscated: 'Human life
e requires a justifica-
the men who will be
w and free democratic
humility before God,
onsibility towards the
act in this spirit then
adequate, and we shall
n Fatherland with hope

been aware that
Government and
and economic
during the visit
nd I think it true
erious misgivings
told the French
on to doubt the
ns with France.
were going on
endanger that
to develop into
onviction – in
r had said on
of France in
of the Saar
to satisfy all

ellor has just
of real and
. Personally
these just
f that at the
lerstand our
50, after the
January. A
conventions
overnment.

33

# The Conditions for Franco-G[ ]
# Understanding*

FOR many months now German public opinion has[ ]
negotiations were proceeding between the French [ ]
the Government of the Saar concerning politica[ ]
developments in the Saar. Discussions took place [ ]
of the French Foreign Minister Robert Schuman, a[ ]
to say that no attempt was made to conceal the s[ ]
all Germans feel in face of this development. I [ ]
Foreign Minister at the time that there was no reaso[ ]
willingness of Germany to engage in direct conversatio[ ]
But I also pointed out that the negotiations which [ ]
between France and the Saar were calculated to [ ]
Franco-German rapprochement which was beginning [ ]
Franco-German friendship. I also expressed the [ ]
which I was only repeating what the Federal Chancell[ ]
a number of previous occasions – that the interests [ ]
the Saar, the interests of Germany, and the interest[ ]
itself, could be accommodated in a way calculated [ ]
parties.

But the agreements of March 3rd, which the Chanc[ ]
made known to the House, must produce a feeling [ ]
profound disappointment in the whole German peopl[ ]
I was even more affected by the reaction abroad [ ]
criticisms and this just resentment. Although I tell mys[ ]
moment one can hardly expect French newspapers to u[ ]

*This speech on the Saar problem was made on March 10t[ ]
visit of the French Foreign Minister Robert Schuman to Bon[ ]
week previously, on March 3rd, the Saar Government had signe[ ]
with the French Government despite the misgivings of the Fed[ ]

34

feelings I must quote a particularly interesting comment by the *Neue Zürcher Zeitung* on March 7th:

> 'The violence of Germany's reaction to the Franco-Saar agreements comes as a surprise to dispassionate circles. The German comments are impelled by such unbridled passion and such a lack of objectivity that non-German circles in Bonn are faced with an incomprehensible phenomenon that can only be explained by the obstinate persistence of resentment against France as "the archenemy".'

On the contrary, I for my part find it difficult to grasp why large sections of the world press should show so little understanding for Germany's feelings; why they fail to sense, in the words of the German Chancellor, the profound anxiety of a man so fully conscious of his obligations, as Chancellor of the German Federal Republic, to co-operate without any secret reservations in the building up of a real European community; why they should have so failed to understand the deep – I would almost say tragic – disappointment we Germans have suffered precisely because we uphold this European idea. No one can accuse the German Federal Government of having failed to make itself the mouthpiece not only of German opinions, but of real European emotions. In complete agreement with the Parties, whose confidence he enjoys, the Chancellor directly approached France months ago, and he did it, I may say, with a determination and courage which very likely surprised some people both inside and outside Germany.

The previous speaker, Doctor Schumacher, was right when he said that courage and daring were necessary to realize the European idea, and that it would be a great mistake to be cunning and evasive. I don't think that one can justly charge the policy of the Chancellor with being evasive. At the same time the Chancellor did not make the matter too simple by merely proposing that we should let bygones be bygones, and not allow the past to affect the present or the future. No! He expressly recognized the French point of view and described the need France feels for real security as a reality which he was very anxious to take into account.

Although Germany's foreign policy is still in the hands of the High Commissioners, the Chancellor was right to make this direct appeal to France; and I think the echo his words found showed him that he did the right thing. Shouldn't he and we be similarly understood

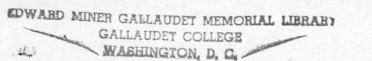

EDWARD MINER GALLAUDET MEMORIAL LIBRARY
GALLAUDET COLLEGE
WASHINGTON, D. C.

now that we are doubly disappointed? Disappointed in particular that our disappointment is not understood?

Before ending the state of war with Germany the Allies made a series of declarations to which the previous speaker has also referred. I do not propose to analyse the character of these declarations from the angle of international law. I will also not discuss how far in the view of the then heads of Allied Governments the German people possess the express right to appeal to these declarations. And, in fact, both questions seem unimportant to me, because I did not have the impression then, and I do not have it now, that these declarations were intended to create new international law. On the contrary, I feel that they were intended to confirm international law as it stood.

The Atlantic Charter of August 14th 1941 declared:

'Their countries seek no aggrandisement, territorial or other. They desire to see no territorial changes that do not accord with the freely expressed wishes of the people concerned. They respect the right of all peoples to choose the form of government under which they will live; and they wish to see sovereign rights and self-government restored to those who have been forcibly deprived of them.'

The Atlantic Charter was clearly recognized by the Government of the French Republic on December 26th 1944.

The report on the Yalta Conference records expressly:

'By this declaration we reaffirm our faith in the principles of the Atlantic Charter, our pledge in the declaration of the United Nations.'

The gist of these declarations from the Atlantic Charter and from the Yalta Conference was subsequently reflected in the Charter of the United Nations of June 26th 1945, which declares that the aim of the organization is to encourage friendly relationships between the nations, based on a respect for the principle of equal rights and the self-determination of peoples. France has also formally accepted the Charter of the United Nations.

I do not wish to raise here the question of whether we already have the written right to appeal to this Charter of the United Nations. I believe that if we are ever to create a new relation between peoples based on the unwritten but sacred principles of law and justice, we should not behave like cunning litigants and try to outwit each other, and we should not try to interpret objective standards from a subjective point of view. By so doing we might not be in the right even if we ultimately made our point. I thought, and I still think, that the Allied nations were serious when they made those declarations and expressed those ideas. But then at least the French Republic should take them into account in its relationship with Germany, and in what it does or leaves undone in the Saar.

I do not propose to repeat what has already been said about the legal position of France towards the Saar. The Memorandum of April 10th 1947 of the French Government to the Moscow Conference contained two specific demands with regard to the Saar, but down to the present day the other Allied Governments have not granted them. When we are now told that this Memorandum justifies the attitude of the French Government then it is interesting to recall what the American Secretary of State Marshall said at that same conference about this Memorandum:

'Returning to the problems of boundaries, I may seem to my colleagues to be unduly emphatic regarding this question. My emphasis comes from a deep sense of responsibility to my country regarding the settlement of this particular issue. Twice in recent years the United States has been compelled to send its military forces across the Atlantic to participate in a war which started in Europe. In men by the million and dollars by the billion we did our best to contribute to the victories for the preservation of a free Europe. Our task is to make a peace settlement which in future years will become, as it were, self-enforcing. We want a peace settlement which will encourage the people of Europe to work together peacefully. We want a settlement that will live and that history will approve. We want above all to avoid a solution which will create a highly explosive situation through congestion and lack of food and other resources essential to modern civilization. We have to look beyond today and tomorrow, to look twenty-five and fifty years ahead of us, beyond the lifetime of most of us.'

I suggest that when referring to this 1947 Memorandum one should not forget these words of the American Secretary of State, particularly as they seem to me to say very much what the previous speaker here said. They strike me as an urgent warning against once more creating peace on any basis but that of law and justice.

We are told that in 1947 the German people in the Saar made a real political decision. But in my view it would be a distortion of what happened in the Saar in the years 1946 and 1947 to pretend that the Landtag elections there had the character of a plebiscite. To claim that these elections represented real political self-determination would be to degrade the high principle of the self-determination of peoples. Quite apart from the fact that the victorious powers have repeatedly declared that any alteration of Germany's 1937 frontiers must be left to a peace treaty, we can certainly say for the honour of the German people in the Saar that they would never freely have approved such a development. No one who has even cursorily read the preamble of the so-called Saar Constitution can possibly say that it recognizes fundamental democratic rights, such as first found their vital expression in France herself. And we are certainly not prepared to agree that a Landtag and the Government of a German Land which came into being as part of a zone of occupation and at the direction of an occupying power, without at the same time losing its character as part and parcel of the German State, have the legal or moral right to conclude such agreements concerning German territory as we now have before us.

I do not wish to go into the details of these agreements again here, and I will confine myself to saying that no matter how you interpret them they could mean the economic, and perhaps even the political severance of a part of Germany from the whole. It is quite true that the declaration handed to the Federal Chancellor yesterday from the French Government is open to various interpretations, and I should certainly not like to agree with the previous speaker, who declared that the French statement spoke merely of the confirmation of the Saar agreements in the peace treaty, which, he feels, means that the agreements are intended to persist beyond the peace treaty and merely require its ratification.

In German interests, and because I accept the sincerity of the French Government's declaration, I prefer to look at things differently, and believe that the agreements have been reached on the understanding that they will automatically lapse unless they are expressly confirmed by a subsequent peace treaty. I feel that this is the only acceptable interpretation, since otherwise the French declaration would have neither political nor moral value.

The Federal Chancellor, and the previous speaker on behalf of the strongest opposition party, both stressed that we are very serious indeed in our desire for European unity, and it should certainly not be forgotten that the German people in particular took up this idea with a seriousness and sincerity beyond all doubt. Perhaps it was under the impression of the utter collapse after a terrible war, and after experiencing the revolting degeneration of an evil and pathological nationalism, and the lying and exaggerated interpretation of a false conception of sovereignty, that the German people were brought to recognize even more than others that a community of people who want peace is the necessary corollary to a community of nations desiring peace.

The declaration of Article 24 of the German Federal Constitution that Germany is willing and ready to transfer sovereign rights to inter-State institutions, and to agree to a limitation of her own sovereignty in the interests of a system of mutual collective security and the establishment of a peaceable and permanent relationship in Europe and between the peoples of the world was no empty gesture. As far as I know no other European constitution contains such a profession of faith in a joint order, such a voluntary renunciation of sovereign rights, such a basis for a real conception of sovereignty.

None of us, of course, has ever been in any doubt that in the harsh realities of politics and economics it will be no easy task to realize the idea of a united Europe. Nevertheless, only twenty-five years ago such ideas were regarded as utopian, and anyone who held them as an impractical idealist, but today we have already taken one essential step in the right direction. The numerous meetings and discussions between European statesmen in recent years have shown that there is a very real desire in all European countries to turn this joint aim into a joint task and to carry it out in sincere co-operation. We are farther advanced today than we were in 1930 when the great Frenchman and European Aristide Briand – the partner of the great German and European Gustav Stresemann – put forward his plan for a united Europe, declaring:

'The work of bringing the nations of Europe together accords with necessities which are sufficiently urgent and vital to give it a purpose in creative work which would, indeed, could, never be directed against anyone.'

We have come closer to the realization of that aim.

Even though the Statute of Europe represents only the first step, it is already impossible to separate it from the political development of recent years, and I feel that we should resist the temptation to study its inadequacies, and concentrate on its real content instead. I am aware that the tasks the Council of Europe has to tackle are hedged around with a sort of casuistry, and that above the Council itself there is – I almost felt inclined to say 'unfortunately' – the Council of Ministers as a mentor. Unfortunately, because those who took part in the first session of the Council of Europe in Strasbourg told me that the dynamic vigour natural to such a council was toned down and repeatedly held in check by that conservatism which is equally natural to Governments. Such criticism, and the disappointment with the first results in Strasbourg, might be summed up in the words of an English representative at the Hague: 'Perhaps we shall have to create Europe with the peoples of Europe against their Governments.'

All the same, I disagree with the previous speaker, who said that the Council of Europe will prevent us from discussing Franco-German problems in Strasbourg, assuming that we come together there. The fact is that the limitations of an organization are created not so much by its own constitution as by the available good-will. No statute, no matter how it is drafted and what restrictions it tries to impose, will prevent Europeans from coming together round a table in Strasbourg to discuss and resolve the problems which interest them. Our approach here must not be sceptical and filled with doubts. We must, as Doctor Schumacher said here, be daring and courageous and not cunning and evasive.

The Council of Europe was preceded by the 1948 Hague Congress, and I don't think anyone who took part in it will ever forget the deep impression made by this first real European gathering. We should be betraying the spirit of Europe if we did not continue in this path. I for one can still remember the speech of Professor Brugmans, one of the pioneers of European unity:

> 'Once again we are called upon to defy a threat; to resist the creation of a colonialized, exploited, totalitarian and subjugated Europe. If we seize this last chance then our children's children will say: they came together in difficulty and suffering but they succeeded in correcting their mistakes and overcoming their weaknesses. They proved that nothing can break the will of free peoples. They did right. They were strong and they served the cause of peace. They were worthy of humanity.'

I recall this memory here because now I want to speak to France;

I want to say to Paris: we regard these agreements you have made as not only a danger to the European idea, but an offence against the spirit of Europe and an offence against the spirit of democracy. The Saar could be and it should be a bridge between France and Germany. But, can't you see that after this Germany must fear that you are building a drawbridge which you intend to raise? Do you really think this is the right line to take if France and Germany are ever to be friends? And it is absolutely necessary that they should be friends if there is ever to be a united Europe.

The Parliamentary Council which adopted the Federal Constitution declared expressly that it was also acting in the name of those Germans who were not in a position to co-operate. Amongst them are those Germans who live in the Saar. Our Constitution calls on all Germans everywhere to bring about the unity and freedom of their country. The Germans living in the Saar are part of this one German people. We want a united Germany in a united Europe, and we hope for a free Germany in a free Europe. We take this freedom seriously, and its authentic expression is political self-determination such as the Atlantic Charter and the Charter of the United Nations both guarantee.

Only a few days ago the American High Commissioner suggested that free elections should be held throughout Germany. But is any part of the German people to be excluded from such free elections and denied the right to make a really democratic decision? We should be bad Europeans if we did not profoundly deplore the agreements of March 3rd and if we failed to lend vigorous support to the solemn protest of the Chancellor.

The Party which I represent here unreservedly approves of the declarations of the Federal Government as presented to us here by the Chancellor, and in particular it accepts his conclusions. It urges him to do what he has proposed, and it assures him that he is supported not only by this Assembly but by the whole German people.

The French writer Saint-Exupéry once said: '*Le plus beau métier d'hommes est d'unir les hommes.*' In this spirit let France now inaugurate talks with Germany. We should not squabble about who is the worst European, but compete in friendly rivalry to see who can be the better.

# 5

# Germany's Contribution to the Defence of Europe*

ON December 16th 1949 I was instructed to make the following declaration in the name of the Coalition Government:

'The German people have been heavily hit by the war and its consequences. They must therefore summon up all their moral and material forces if they are to renew their political existence and reconstruct their economy so that all citizens may enjoy sound and healthy conditions of life. We are still hoping that, having won the war, the victorious powers will ultimately succeed in winning the peace. A new war would bury all the hopes of the German people for good. They have therefore no thought of rearmament. In accordance with her constitution, Germany, which is territorially and historically a part of Western civilization, wants to serve the peace of the world and the freedom of mankind as a free and equal member of a united Europe.'

In the months that have passed since this declaration was made it has lost nothing of its validity, but nothing shows more urgently and, if I may say so, more unfortunately, the crisis facing our world than the fact that we are now compelled to discuss whether, and under what circumstances, Germany should be prepared to play a part in the defence of our joint European freedom.

In discussing this question we should follow the example of the Chancellor of the Reich, and remember the need for peace. I think it is no exaggeration to say that the disasters of the two world wars fell particularly heavily on the Germans, more so than on any other

*Speech in the German Federal Diet on November 8th 1950 on a governmental declaration concerning Germany's contribution to the defence of Europe.

people anywhere. This morning Doctor Schumann quoted terrible figures to this effect. For this reason no one would have the right to be astonished if the reaction of the German people is not an immediate and enthusiastic assent. But when we repeatedly and solemnly express our desire for peace – because we are well aware that without peace we could not possibly carry out the many tasks that the past has left us and the present places before us – and when we say that no sacrifice is too great for us in the cause of peace, let no one doubt the sincerity of our assurance.

When I now preface my remarks with a sincere wish for the preservation of peace, and when I say that we regret nothing more keenly than the necessity to enter into such a discussion in the first place, I must also say that it would be foolish and dangerous to close our eyes to the facts – not only those of the immediate past – and pretend that Germany is in no danger and that the existence of the Federal Republic is not threatened. We cannot ward off peril by burying our heads in the sand. It is our duty to look facts in the face, and I for one welcome this discussion, which was absolutely necessary because more than one thoughtless declaration has been made in public and some misgivings have been felt. I also have the impression that sometimes comments have been made before the commentator gave himself time to think of the full implication of his words – sometimes even before the text of what was commented on was actually available. I think we should all have done better – and I am making no exceptions – if we had spoken with a little more forethought and consideration, if we had remembered that millions of our fellow countrymen would follow such a debate with the keenest attention, and that therefore any false note, any slip of the tongue, might well cast millions of people into renewed anxiety. I listened very closely to what Doctor Schumacher had to say, and I can assure him that his objections and his qualifications are largely ours too. I feel that we should be very frank about these matters since such a discussion can help to clear the air.

If I am to sum up my general impression of the debate then I think I may say confidently that the great majority of this House, like the great majority of the German people, is well aware of the seriousness of the situation and is inwardly ready to make a contribution to the defence of its freedom, because it knows only too well that it cannot live without freedom.

We should not let ourselves be influenced in so vital a matter by the moralizing or lecturing of others, and we certainly should not allow a newspaper article to scare us. I think it would be unfair to the American people if we judged their attitude from one article in the *Neue Zeitung*. A speech made by the President of the United States a few weeks ago on the fifth anniversary of the founding of the United Nations Organization is a much better source. It was a speech informed by a deep moral earnestness, and one that I think everyone of us here would be prepared to echo in full. Allow me to quote one passage:

'I believe the people of the world rely on two great purposes. They look to it to help them improve the conditions under which they live. And they rely on it to fulfil their profound longing for peace. These two purposes are closely interwoven. Without peace, it is impossible to make lasting progress toward a better life for all. Without progress in human welfare, the foundations of peace will be insecure. That is why we can never afford to neglect one of these purposes at the expense of the other.'

I certainly don't think there is any false moralizing here. It says what we are all glad to hear. And in particular it says very clearly that you cannot separate domestic and foreign security.

We can make a decisive contribution to the preservation of peace by doing our utmost to give the German people a feeling of domestic security, and by improving their living standards so that they will become more and more immune to the poison from the East. All the same it would be very short-sighted to suppose, as some intellectuals apparently do, that this is all we need do as our contribution to peace. Let me remind you of something Friedrich Naumann said a good many years ago: 'What use is the finest social legislation if the Cossacks come?'

Nevertheless I am absolutely in agreement with Doctor Schumacher when he says that we should not exploit the anxiety with which people look fearfully to the East, and I can assure him that we have no intention of letting our decisions be influenced by any such anxiety neurosis. We shall do just what we feel necessary to help preserve peace and maintain our freedom.

There has been some discussion here as to whether Germany, the German Federal Republic, has already declared herself ready to make a contribution to general security – even whether she has a right to or not. In particular some criticism has been caused because official utterances seem already to have expressed such willingness. Let us be quite clear on one point straight away: we are not being asked what we are prepared to do for war. Indeed, the only thing that comes into question for us at all is: what are we prepared to do for peace? In my opinion the answer to this question should be: everything!

I should like to say a word or two in particular about the attitude of the people of Berlin. At a time when millions of people outside that city had already given up hope, and were beginning to feel that further resistance would be useless; at a time when many people, who have, incidentally, since recovered their courage, were beginning to whisper that perhaps the time had come for us to abandon the 'experiment', those millions of Germans who have their homes in Berlin did not lose their courage. They just went on with their heroic resistance, and they proved thereby to the whole German people and to world public opinion that there are again Germans in the world who value freedom above all else. Their courageous attitude has already borne fruit. If I may reinforce the remarks of Doctor Schumacher, sacrifices were made for other things apart from South Korea. The first sacrifices were made by Americans for the freedom of Berlin, including the loss of human lives.

Of course we are not going to let ourselves be guided by any kind of obsession that something must now be done at once, even though some of the speeches here and certain newspaper articles seem to suggest just that. We are not so much interested in doing something, as in doing the right thing. And, although the remarks of Doctor Schumacher might have suggested it, I do not agree that the discussion here is between out-and-out and qualified re-armers.

To begin with, can't we abandon the use of the wretched term 're-militarize'? Particularly as it has very disagreeable associations for the general public, and suggests that we intend to restore, or at least copy, the past. For myself and my friends I can say with all possible emphasis that we intend to do neither the one thing nor the other. On the contrary, we firmly intend to create something new. We do not want re-militarization; we do not want a national German army as an instrument of power-politics. What we want is to make a contribution to a European army as part of the integration of Europe. We want to perform the same tasks and undertake the same obligations within such a European community as everyone else. Not re-militarization but an appeal to the German people to preserve

45

their freedom and co-operate in such a joint army. I can see no contradiction with our constitution here.

I should like to quote a remark which seems to suggest that there were also individual Social Democrat members of the Parliamentary Council who could clearly foresee the situation which has arisen today. As a member of the drafting committee I was instructed to propose that the word 'war' in Article 26 should be replaced by the term 'war of aggression', and speaking on behalf of the committee I said: 'Aggressive warfare is forbidden, not defensive warfare surely?'

Our colleague Schmid then spoke in favour of retaining the word 'war', and these were his reasons:

> 'We should make it very clear that there is just no further room in an ordered community of peoples for what was once regarded as the *ultima ratio regum*, as the supreme sovereign right; that should it ever become necessary to use force then it should not be used as an act of national sovereignty, but as an act of collective security by all nations anxious to preserve world peace; and that it must be made impossible for aggressors to disturb it.'

I hardly think it would be possible to put the present attitude of the Federal Government more clearly and succinctly than these wise and pregnant observations made two years ago. I have already made it clear here that we are not interested in creating a new national army, and I propose to repeat here the decisive statement I made on behalf of my friends in Strasbourg, which still applies:

> 'In order to preserve peace and maintain the freedom of the democratic peoples of Europe and the world my friends are ready and determined to support the idea, not of a national army, but of a united European army of free and equal democratic peoples under joint European leadership and democratic control. In voting for Mr Churchill's resolution we desire, though Germany has not yet freedom of action, to make it clear that we feel ourselves just as much under an obligation to defend freedom and justice as the representatives of the other European peoples.'

I think this covers all those qualifications with regard to such participation that Doctor Schumacher expressed here. As a condition for our participation in the defence of the Western world he required unconditional approval of the principle of international solidarity. I agree with him absolutely, and I should like to recall the communiqué of the Foreign Ministers' Conference on September 19th 1950, which declared that the Allied Governments would regard any attack on the Federal Republic, or on Berlin, from whatever side it might come, as an attack upon themselves. In my view this is a declaration of international solidarity such as we should hardly have dared to hope for only a few months ago. I quite understand – indeed, I share – the anxiety induced by the fact that in the event of a conflict, which I hope we may be spared, Germany is, on account of her geographical situation, more endangered than any other country.

But no guarantees and no promises can alter the geographical situation of our Fatherland or change the frontiers within which we suffer today. Of course we sincerely hope that Germany will never become a battlefield again. But perhaps we should direct this appeal to international solidarity and our desire that no one should play with the idea of Germany's being turned into a cockpit of war, to the French Defence Minister, Jules Moch, who is unfortunately a Socialist.

When Doctor Schumacher demands that one country should not be misused to defend another, I can only agree with him in this too. I am sure that none of us really believes that German troops would be used under any pretext or under any circumstances for wrong purposes. But when we demand that one country should not be used to defend another, then this must surely involve an acknowledgement that we should at least take part in the defence of our own country, for how otherwise could we make such demands of others? Let me utter a warning against the idea which has been put forward, though not here today, that because we surrendered unconditionally we can now afford to say: 'You beat us, now take the consequences and defend us.' Now, of course, no one proposes to relieve of their responsibility those who undertook precisely this for Germany after her unconditional surrender, but nevertheless we really cannot thrust our hands into our pockets and expect others to defend us on the Elbe, and perhaps on the Oder-Neisse line tomorrow. Such an attitude might well be misunderstood. I also fear that it might lead to a loss of confidence in us because it might be thought that there were once again people in Germany playing with the idea that an alliance with the East might one day be more favourable. This would do our credibility and reputation no good at all.

I also agree with what has been said here by a number of speakers: namely, that the most important condition of our policy must be

47

that we first build up a sound social order at home, that we should create social conditions which will make life worth while for the man who works for his living, because only then can we expect him to be prepared to fight to defend the State and the social order in which he lives. And he will believe in it and fight for it only if it is just. I repeat: we have no intention of paring down social security, and the anxiety expressed here is unfounded. On the other hand, we cannot hope to maintain it unless we are ready to defend the conditions which make it possible.

I can quite understand the fear that if Germany takes part in the defence of Europe and the world it will involve material sacrifices, and that our living standards will suffer in consequence. At the same time we should surely misunderstand our mission if at any time in the future we made Soviet Russia a present of the country with the highest standard of living in Europe because of our unwillingness to defend it.

The question of the occupation costs has been very properly raised in this connection. I quite agree that the occupation costs Germany is paying, and the extent to which they contribute to keeping troops on a war footing ready to defend the peace and security of Europe, already represent a financial contribution on Germany's part to our joint defence. I therefore regard it as a matter of course that this point of view should be stressed in the negotiations which are about to take place on this question.

A certain amount of astonishment has been expressed here that the Federal Government should regard the recent declaration of the French Premier, Monsieur Pléven, as a valuable step towards the integration of Europe. The truth is, of course, that none of us entirely approved of it, and it was certainly criticized. In particular I regret that the French Government should have attempted to link up the Schuman plan with the possibility of establishing such a European Army, since to do so might well tend to create the impression that there was an intention to exercise pressure on the course of the negotiations. On the other hand I feel that it would be wrong to stress merely the negative side of the declaration, because there are passages which express just what we too desire; for example, its conclusion:

'France had already decided to do her share manfully in the efforts to establish a joint defence within the framework of the Atlantic Community. Today she takes the initiative with a constructive proposal to establish a united Europe. Europe must not forget the lessons of the Second World War, and at a time when Europe is beginning to renew its forces it must be so organized that its strength can never be used but to serve the defence of international security and the cause of peace.'

When I read this passage I must agree with the Federal Government that here we have a real and valuable contribution to the integration of Europe.

And now to a point which the Federal Chancellor himself has also raised: namely, what attitude Germany should take to the proposals for the pacification of Europe and the restoration of German unity which have been put forward by the Kremlin. Personally I think there isn't very much to say, and though we heard a representative of the extreme Left in this House solemnly declare that the document in which they were contained was the most important the world has seen since the end of the war I will not hold it against him – after all, that's what he's sent here to say. But there is nothing new in that document, and therefore I find it a little difficult to understand his enthusiasm. This House has already demanded that the German people living in all the four zones of occupation should be allowed free and secret elections. If we were offered a guarantee of general, direct, equal, secret and free elections then I am quite certain that none of us here would dream of not accepting the result of such a vote of the German people. There is just one further condition I should like to add to such a guarantee: namely, that the man who freely gives his vote should not be called to account for his action at a later date.

If this were to happen then we should find ourselves in the happy situation of being able to dissolve this House in accordance with Article 146 of the Constitution, which provides that it shall lose its validity on the day the German people are once again in a position to decide their fate by a free vote. But until that day comes I do not think we should shirk our responsibility for any reason whatsoever – on the ground perhaps that our authority is inadequate. Indeed, it would be a very grave matter if we sought to avoid a clear and definite attitude. But there is one thing I should like to make clear: if anyone says that the question we are now discussing was not on the agenda when the Federal Landtag was elected and that therefore the Landtag has no authorization to deal with it on behalf of the

German people, then logic demands that he should keep his mouth shut altogether, since by the same token his electors have given him no mandate to discuss it at all.

Let me finally say one thing in all seriousness. Our experiences in the past and what we have achieved in recent years not only justify our heartfelt desire for the preservation of peace, but impose an obligation on us all to do what we can to that end. You have only to recall the year 1945 when, apathetic from the shock of an unprecedented collapse, the German people seemed at the end of their tether. Then, look back on the five years that have passed since. The German people worked with admirable industry and a high sense of duty to build up a new Germany, and many now envy us our achievements. Surely these five years of creative labour impose an obligation on us to preserve their fruits? Let us not forget that once they had lost their freedom the German people had to make enormous efforts and sacrifices to win it back again. And we all know that if ever we lost our freedom again we should never recover it. We realize, too, that there can be no peace without freedom, no democracy without freedom, and no justice without freedom. And what human dignity can there be unless it is protected in freedom?

It was no easy task to build up what we can see before us today. We are still at the beginning of our labours, and anything that disturbed us now would be very damaging indeed. But it is not just a question of avoiding interruptions. We are faced with clear alternatives: do we want to live on in freedom, or do we feel that we are no longer up to our great task and would sooner abandon it?

I am quite certain that not only the great majority of this House but also of the German people are prepared to do everything possible to preserve peace and to defend the freedom of their State, which is based on respect for the rights of man. They will surely also agree that internal and external peace is indivisible. We therefore regard it as our imperative task to continue working with all our might to improve living standards and further social development as part of Germany's reconstruction, and at the same time to co-operate in her external defence.

We have noted with gratification that the opposition speakers have also declared themselves ready to co-operate with the other free peoples of the world for the defence of freedom and the preservation of peace; but the majority of the House deeply regrets that tactical considerations have been allowed to hamper, if not prevent, the

Federal Landtag from going forward unitedly towards this aim. We are completely in agreement with the Government that an appropriate German contribution to the preservation of peace must depend categorically on the granting of both equal rights and equal obligations where the German people are concerned. We feel that the international solidarity which is absolutely necessary for the maintenance of peace and the preservation of freedom should include practical solidarity with the German people, and ultimately it will do so. We are certainly willing to play our part in bringing it about. At the same time we cannot but express our anxiety because we feel that the methods proposed by the chairman of the Social Democratic Party militate against the attainment of this aim, and that for this reason they endanger our common objective.

We appeal to the German people not to allow themselves to become embittered in the struggle for the attainment of this aim either by memories or resentments, whether justified or not. We appeal to the German people not to let themselves be intimidated either by fear or threats, but to go forward with determination together with the other free peoples of the world for the preservation of peace and the maintenance of freedom.

# 6

# The Schuman Plan and European Co-operation*

IN his declaration on behalf of the Government last Wednesday the Federal Chancellor pointed out that almost all the reservations and conditions expressed during the debate on the first reading, and summarized in particular in your resolution, had become invalid since then. I can only refer to this statement and the material made available to the House by the Foreign Office.

This makes it even more difficult to understand why a section of this House says: very well, the Ruhr authority will cease to operate, the coal and steel control groups will disappear, the limits on capacity and production in the steel industry will go too, and the security authorities will no longer interfere with our coal and steel trade. Granted; but there are other burdens and impositions which we have inherited from defeat, and therefore we reject the Schuman plan because not all these hindrances are to be removed before its ratification. Such an attitude strikes me as unrealistic and unobjective, and those who adopt it do not seem to understand just what the Schuman plan does mean.

We do not approve of the agreement because we think that to sign it with the five other participating countries will serve Germany instead of a peace treaty, which, for reasons known to us all, we do not, for the time being, wish to see concluded, and on this point the great majority of this assembly is undoubtedly agreed. We are also not signing the agreement in order to replace some restrictions by others – on the contrary, we have made our signing depend on the abolition of all restrictions, reservations and interference which still

*Speech delivered during the debate in the Federal Landtag on January 11th 1952 on the agreement to form the European Coal and Steel Community.

one-sidedly affect our heavy industries as a result of our living under occupation law. We have never ceased to insist that only partners with equal rights and equal obligations should be members of the community. If it is objected that these restrictions and so on would in all probability disappear on their own at some time or other without our bothering to sign the agreement, I must admit that this is very likely true. On the other hand, does anyone really believe that we have so much time in hand, and that our position in Europe and the world is so secure that we can reasonably afford to say: yes, we are prepared to enter into discussions concerning international co-operation, but only after, in the course of years, perhaps many years, a *de facto* situation is reached in which all the restrictions imposed on us as a result of the lost war have practically ceased to exist?

I repeat: we are not signing the Schuman plan because it improves our economic and political position, but because we regard the basic idea of close co-operation between all European States as a good one. At the same time we welcome it in the economic and political interests of Germany. The absolute condition for our signature was, of course, the re-establishment of full equality within the framework of the agreement. If all the Schuman plan did was to bring about the abolition of the restrictions I have mentioned sooner than would otherwise have been the case, then this alone would be sufficient reason to support it in the interests of the German people.

My friend Etzel spoke in favour of the resolution submitted by the Coalition Government, and while completely in agreement with his remarks I should like to add one request to the Federal Government; namely, that as soon as this House and the Federal Council have ratified the agreement they should open up the necessary negotiations for the establishment of the High Authority. Germany's economic policy as a whole requires that the organizations to be established by the European Coal and Steel Community should begin to operate immediately after the agreement becomes valid. All outstanding questions should be settled without delay in discussions between the participating countries. The seat of the High Authority remains to be chosen, and all arrangements must be made in advance to ensure that the High Authority can begin its operations with an adequate staff as soon as possible. It is also important that the contracting parties should come to some agreement now, if possible, on the composition of the High Authority, that the eight members should be appointed without delay, and that they should then immediately co-opt the ninth member.

All these arrangements can and should be made now – even if ratification of the agreement by some of the participating countries is still outstanding – because delay in settling the preliminaries is undesirable and would be damaging not only to Germany's interests but to all others. In particular, decisions which will henceforth be the responsibility of the High Authority must not come too late through any failure to get it working in good time, as this might mean that the Ruhr Authority would have to step in again for the second quarter of 1952. This is why it is important to complete the necessary arrangements in good time. The first decisions of the High Authority will clearly be of particular political and even psychological importance, and its preliminary activities will be studied with very close attention indeed – and that not only in Germany but in all the countries concerned. This is why I feel that the Ministerial Council should be formed now.

The significance of Statute No. 27 in relation to the Schuman plan was discussed here this morning. Neither the Federal Chancellor nor I could understand how a member of this House, and a lawyer at that, could say that Statute No. 27 bore the character of an international agreement and was therefore binding on the High Authority of the Schuman plan. Now quite apart from the fact that I believe this interpretation to be fundamentally false – even the member himself, who happens to be chairman of the Foreign Affairs Committee, must know that the Federal Government has never come to any arrangement concerning Statute No. 27 – I really don't see any necessity, if there is any doubt, for 'the authentic interpretation' as the opposition understands it, to be given to the House.

The frequently quoted declaration of the French Foreign Minister in Paris can make no difference to this. Colleague Ollenhauer says that the declaration is of great importance because it could mean an interpretation of the agreement. But even a French Foreign Minister can be wrong in a matter of detail, and, then, he is opposed by the clear and definite statement of the Federal Chancellor. Further, if you care to read the letter of the French High Commissioner M. François Poncet as the representative of the Allied High Commission, which is with the material submitted by the Foreign Office, you will see that there is not a word in it about any agreement between the three Allied Powers and the Federal Government, but merely about the administration of Statute No. 27, which was, as the Federal Chancellor has pointed out, imposed on us, so that the Federal Government has always refused to co-operate in order not to create the impression that it recognizes its legal validity.

We certainly desire that the Allied Governments should now keep the promises they have made to us. The controls imposed on our coal and steel industries should be abrogated as soon as the Schuman plan comes into operation. The preparatory work – for which, after all, six years were available – must now be concluded at last in order that the new status for Germany's heavy industries announced by the Allies from 1945 on should finally be brought into being. I hardly think it is unfair criticism to suggest that with the very large staff the Allies have had at their disposal they might well have shown a little more celerity in dealing with these problems but for the force of inertia which seems to reside in all institutional bodies.

We now desire the Federal Government to make it quite clear to the Allies that the time has really come for them to accelerate the winding up of Statute No. 27, and that henceforth no further difficulties of a formal nature should be raised. Statute No. 27 has three quite clearly defined aims: to prevent and break up economic concentrations, to prevent the development of any capacity to wage war, and to eliminate the notorious supporters of the Third Reich and its aggressive plans.

It is now high time that clearly-defined conditions and definite responsibilities should be created in the industries concerned. It has been pointed out, for example, that what has proved useful in the coal-mining industry – the so-called Unoactu establishment of new companies – is frowned upon in the iron and steel industries. This is probably only because someone else is in charge there. And perhaps, too, because it is possible to find a more complicated solution. In any case, I sincerely hope that the Federal Government will do its best to secure the acceleration of these final operations; and that in particular it will insist to the Allied High Commission, and if necessary to the Allied Governments, that the Schuman plan cannot possibly work smoothly unless there is a very clear division of tasks, definite responsibilities, and clearly defined competences throughout the industries.

This morning the Opposition complained that the Federal Chancellor had suggested that to be in favour of the Schuman plan was to be in favour of a united Europe, and that to be against it was to be against a united Europe; and my colleague Ollenhauer protested in particular against this over-simplification, and indignantly rejected any suggestion that his party was not in favour of a united Europe.

I must point out, however, that in a speech broadcast from Frankfurt a week ago – and again here today – Ollenhauer himself did the over-simplifying by saying that to be in favour of the Schuman plan was to be against German reunification. I certainly don't care for such over-simplification. It startles me and fills me with misgivings – particularly as it seems to have arisen only during the past few weeks. But the Social Democratic Party does not lack information and expert advice, so how did it come about that it did not discover until a few weeks back that to accept the Schuman plan would compromise the cause of German reunification?

It was pointed out to our colleague Schmid yesterday that when he spoke on behalf of the Social Democratic Party on July 12th 1951 on a first reading he made no such suggestion. And neither did his Party friend Henssler. After listening to the impassioned arguments of these two speakers today it is difficult to understand how such very great dangers should have escaped their notice then.

And our colleague Schmid, it should be remembered, was a member of the Parliamentary Council. Together with the great majority of the Council he was emphatically in favour of Article 24, which provided for the transfer of sovereign rights. This was embodied in a Constitution whose provisional character we all realized, and which, indeed, we stressed by the adoption of Article 146. Those of us, including myself, who co-operated in the drafting of the Constitution had a very good idea of what we were doing, and I think I can say that none of us supposed for one moment that the integration of Germany into Europe by means of Article 24 could in any way compromise the cause of German reunification. Had we done so then quite clearly we should never have adopted it, since the tragic fact of Germany's dismemberment was no secret to us at the time. And even if you could suppose that it was a secret to us it was certainly not to the Governments of the Länder, yet each recommended its Landtag to accept the Article. It was also, of course, known to them when they adopted the Constitution, including Article 24 – incidentally, with help of the votes of the Social Democratic Party. If the Opposition now really thinks that to use Article 24 will endanger the cause of German reunification why did they accept it in the first place?

It is also less difficult to understand how it came about that on May 10 last year Colleague Nölting declared at the Advisory Meeting of the Council of Europe in Strasbourg that his party rejected the Schuman plan not because it went too far but because it did not go far enough. His party, he assured us, demanded real integration throughout the economy; and, if possible, politically too. There wasn't a word about any danger to the cause of German reunification. Is it therefore unfair to ask why they regard a lesser degree of integration in one sphere only as such a great danger to reunification?

Now and again I suspect that they are themselves aware of the ambiguity of their position. In a discussion of a somewhat similar nature only a few weeks ago at the Advisory Meeting in Strasbourg, Colleague Schmid said that he was opposed to a 'Little Europe' solution because he was afraid that a part solution would hamper the full solution, if not make it altogether impossible. An interrupter pointed out how illogical his standpoint was, and asked him to prove his point. He replied by saying that the 'Little German' solution had, in fact, once prevented a full German solution. I can only say that when a jurist of the calibre of our colleague Schmid talks like that it suggests that he is not altogether convinced by his own argument, for, surely, if there is a more convincing example of the fact that a part solution need not prevent, and can actually facilitate, the subsequent whole solution, than the German Zollverein mentioned by Colleague Etzel, I can't think of it. If anyone really believes that this 'Little German' solution made the more embracing solution impossible I can only recommend him to go back to his history books.

Yesterday Professor Nölting said here that the debate in the French National Assembly revealed no trace of European spirit, and that it was conducted with 'a carving knife'. I am startled and dismayed that Professor Nölting should have thought it desirable to use such strong language. Let me therefore quote, as an example of the European spirit Professor Nölting found so conspicuously absent, what M. Schuman himself said in that same debate:

'Our two nations, which have been separated for a very long time by bloody conflicts, are, we may take it, not yet ready for immediate co-operation. Too many incidents, particularly in the past few months, have shown us how many sore points there still are and how much mistrust there still is despite the great progress which really has been attained by men of good will. For this reason we feel sure that the best way to attain rapid success is for France and Germany to work together in a multilateral community in which particularist urges would gradually disappear thanks to constant contact between the participants. In this way the problem of Europe would be raised unobtrusively but necessarily with the problem of Germany. All the world is talking about this new Europe, but no one finds it easy to describe it clearly. By founding this community we are not, it is true, creating this new Europe, but we are quite certainly taking a step towards it.'

I could add many more such quotations for the benefit of Professor Nölting, but I will content myself with one. A young French Deputy, M. Faure, said:

'Thus the working of this community will depend primarily on the goodwill of the people concerned. This is the classic fate of all institutions. They are worth just as much as the spirit that informs them. The fact is that unless we give up our inferiority complex towards Germany right from the start then it would certainly be useless and perhaps even dangerous to take part in any such undertaking.'

Our colleague Ollenhauer has said that he and his friends do not want to introduce any anti-French spirit into the debate. I can only say that in my view there is more European spirit in the speeches I have quoted – and I could quote many others – than in Ollenhauer's suggestion that you could compare the European Coal and Steel Community with the occupation of the Ruhr. And I really can't see much European spirit in the suggestion that the only obviously worse thing than the European Coal and Steel Community would have been an agreement with the Soviet Union.

The fact is, I had the impression that it was Professor Nölting who brandished the carving knife in an attempt to kill the European idea. But the knife wasn't sharp enough, and those he picked to help him were not effective enough. If Professor Nölting really thinks that the Schuman plan is a continuation of the brutal policy of occupation at the expense of the German people then how does he explain that all his Socialist friends in the other countries affected by that plan have voted in its favour? And if he is logical ought he not now to refuse to co-operate internationally any longer with people who seek to extend the brutal policy of occupation for ever?

Professor Nölting tried to make our flesh creep yesterday when he said that 'they' could cut off our supplies and clamp down a sort of economic martial law. It was all very dramatic, and it was very amusing to compare it with the comment of the well-known French communist newspaper *Humanité* on December 28th 1951 on the same set of facts. It was published under the headline 'Ruhr magnates lay hands on Paris gas supply!'

I could produce many quotations from the debate in the French National Assembly to show that the objections put forward here by the Social Democratic Party to the Schuman plan were put forward there by the representatives of heavy industry and the Communists, but I will content myself with a few of the more important voices. General Aumeran, an independent, declared:

'If the European Coal and Steel Community and the European Army is accepted by parliament then France will lose her position as a great nation. It will be impossible for her to maintain her sovereignty over the territory of the French Union.'

Pierre André, of the extreme Right, put the point even more clearly:

'Why have the Germans signed? Let me remind you that we have made the Germans a real present by abolishing our own customs barriers. . . . We have opened our country freely to German coal and German steel, and not only France but our overseas territories too.'

And listen to Professor Perroux of the University of Paris:

'Germany is striving through the European Coal and Steel Community to obtain first economic and then political hegemony in Europe. It is obvious that with her industry, her labour power and her creative energy she is striving to become the leading power in Europe.'

But the time is growing short so let me give you just one more quite short quotation from the *Neue Zürcher Zeitung* on the ratification by the French Chamber:

'The representatives of heavy industry joined hands with the representatives of traditional French security policy against Germany, and used their arguments. But both groups together could not greatly strengthen the opposition to the European Coal and Steel Community. The fact that the economically powerful heavy industry suffered such a clear defeat shows how well founded Schuman's European initiative is; and, in addition, it rebuts the contention of the Left that the political abuse of economic power can be prevented only by nationalization.'

Professor Nölting also threatened us with a mass emigration of Germany's workers. But would it really be such a bad thing if the agreement increased the mobility of the working man? May I remind Professor Nölting and his friends that in Strasbourg they voted for mobility of labour? For me the freedom of a man to go elsewhere is a matter of course and I don't think Europe should continue to impose an export duty on labour-power. And when an official of the IG Metal Union recommended German workers to go and look for work in France during a strike I can't remember hearing Professor Nölting's voice raised in warning.

Colleague Mommer raised the Saar question, and I must say I found it difficult to understand what he was getting at. He kept saying that the Federal Government had failed to play its trump cards, but he didn't tell us what those cards were. In any case, I'm afraid that if we started playing cards with the other powers too much would depend on mere chance. But let me ask Colleague Mommer instead: would it settle the Saar problem if we didn't ratify the Schuman plan? Would it make a settlement more difficult or more easy? I feel strongly that a settlement of the Saar problem will be facilitated by the Schuman plan, when we have concentrated all the economic potential of the six countries, including that of France and Germany, in the European Coal and Steel Community. In view of such a decision it is greatly to be regretted that French foreign policy still seems to regard the Saar as a sort of pledge, as a guarantee of certain security requirements, which I for one feel quite sure are completely out of date anyway. As we have said more than once, all of us here deeply regret that, acting under the emotions of the years 1945–6, which, though understandable enough perhaps, should never have been allowed to lead to political decisions, France has created conditions in the Saar that we cannot possibly accept or recognize. Our refusal to do so is not based on any narrow-minded nationalism, nor is it impelled by any false national pride. It is solely due to our belief that the relations between peoples can rest securely only on a basis of justice. At the same time we do feel that the situation France has created in the Saar not only violates the canons of international law, but is, in addition, morally unjustifiable, whilst at the same time it unquestionably compromises good relations between our two countries.

It is quite clear – and it can be seen from the exchange of correspondence appended to the agreement – that the Federal Government and the coalition parties never for one moment considered recognizing the *de facto* situation which exists in the Saar today as *de jure*, and that we shall never cease to insist with all possible emphasis that the present situation is unjust and should be remedied, particularly because its continued existence must compromise, poison, and endanger the good relations of all the free peoples of Europe. This is the meaning of our motion. Colleague Mommer is afraid that it misses the essential point, but I cannot agree. In fact I cannot help feeling that he has misunderstood Point One, as otherwise he could not possibly have said what he did. One essential thing we must all demand, and that is that freedom should be restored to the Saar. Once this is done we really needn't bother our heads about what the decision of the German people living in the Saar will be.

Speaking in the debate yesterday, our colleague Veit said something which I deplore and cannot possibly let pass. He contended that we are unfairly exploiting the memory of those who died in two world wars in order that we might make up in sentiment what we lack in objective argument. He then went on to say that the memory of the dead was too sacred to him and his friends to allow such an exploitation. As it happens, similar tones were heard in the debate in the French Chamber. General Aumeran, an extreme nationalist, used similarly emotionally-charged words to attack the Schuman plan. He, too, appealed to the memory of the dead of the two world wars, and warned the French Government and the Chamber against forgetting them by ratifying the agreement. The French Prime Minister, M. Pléven, replied: 'Nos morts, mon général, ne sont pas morts pour que tout recommence comme avant.' Personally I cannot feel that anyone who recalls the senseless sacrifices of those wars in that way is in any way besmirching the memory of the dead. In fact I would go so far as to say – and I am inclined to think that you will agree with me – that if we had been so far advanced in Europe twenty-five years ago as to ratify a Schuman plan then the millions who died in the years 1939 to 1945 would never have needed to die at all.

My colleague Ollenhauer and other speakers in the debate put forward a number of cogent points, which we have, in fact, not failed to consider. Indeed, we have thought about them in long months of very careful consideration, but we have come to the conclusion that such misgivings should not prevent us from voting in favour of the plan. We do not want to look at everything through rose-tinted spectacles, and to believe that the day the High Authority begins its work will mean the dawn of a new era of happiness and peace for all. We realize that the new organization will have to stand some pretty severe tests. We are also very well aware that it will function properly only if it is inspired by a true European spirit, and only if the High Authority acts as a supra-national body keenly conscious of its great and unique task to take decisions beyond national frontiers and beyond narrow nationalist conceptions, decisions which will, after all, directly affect 150 million people.

Unlike our colleague Ollenhauer I do not think that the result of our voting in the second reading yesterday was merely, as he put it, a triumph of figures. As democrats we must surely admit that the weight of argument also expresses itself in the power of figures. I don't think they would like it at all if they were in the majority and we said anything like that. And I for one certainly would not say it. I don't think the German people will say it either, and I am convinced that they, including very many of those who voted for the Opposition, do not agree with some of the things that have been said here.

I am firmly convinced that the overwhelming majority of the German people supports the general idea even if they do not understand all the details of a very complicated proposal. They support the idea because millions of people on both sides of the frontier want something more than talk about Europe; they want to see something done about it. What is the use of mere talk? We have had plenty of it here and we had plenty of it in Strasbourg. In fact the President of the Advisory Meeting, Paul-Henri Spaak – incidentally, a Socialist – was so disappointed by so much talk and so little action that he resigned; and in doing so I may say that he was expressing the feelings of millions of ordinary people throughout Europe.

Speaking for myself and my friends, I feel very proud that we were able to co-operate in bringing about this first work of real European integration, and that we had the privilege of laying the first stone in the European foundation. I am under no illusions and I have no utopia in mind, but I feel sure that the inevitability – which our colleague Schmid so fears – of the developments opened up by this first step will lead ultimately not only to the real integration of the free peoples of Europe, but also to the re-unification of Germany herself.

# 7

# The German Agreement and the European Political Community*

THE attitude of the Christian Democrats and of the Christian Social Union to the two agreements now before us was made quite clear during the second reading. Nevertheless, I should like to enumerate once more the chief points which have persuaded us to accept these agreements. I should also like to say that in the meantime we have found our attitude confirmed, and that the reasons which prompted it now seem even stronger to us.

If we had not lived through the past it might be right to judge these two agreements purely from a present-day angle, but, in fact, they must be regarded as a phase of Germany's whole policy as expounded by the Federal Chancellor in his declaration of September 20th 1949. Since then this policy has been persistently followed, and, I think I may say, with undeniable success. There can be no one here who has forgotten that even now we are living under an occupation statute, though, once again thanks to the adroit and consistent policy of the Federal Government, it has been modified in many important particulars, and is, in fact, already something of a dead letter. When the occupation statute was promulgated it represented a bulwark against arbitrariness and it limited the discretionary powers of the occupation authorities. At the time, therefore, it represented a step forward, and as such it was welcomed by all Germans. Nevertheless, the aim of any responsible German policy must necessarily be to free Germany from this dependence and these restrictions. The agreement which is now before us has been drawn up with this same object in view.

*Speech delivered on March 19th 1953 at the third reading of the agreement on the relations between the German Federal Republic and the three Western Powers, and of the agreement establishing the European Defence Community.

None of us here is likely to approve of all its details, and certainly none of us would think of greeting its ratification with enthusiasm. It reminds us too clearly of the catastrophe which accompanied the departure of a horrible régime from the stage. At the same time it led a defeated and dismembered people, who had only just emerged from slavery, into a new phase of dependence. Only the politically naïve could possibly expect that such an agreement could undo what had been done. To demand that it should would be presumption or demagogy, and we should be very foolish if we attempted to indulge in either. However, on the whole, and if we are prepared to accept it in the same spirit of conciliation which informs it, this agreement is not only the best possible in the circumstances, but a really favourable solution in its own right. The Federal Landtag and the whole German people have cause to be grateful to those who helped to bring it about. I regard it as my duty to express these thanks publicly and with the special support of the Federal Chancellor.

The aim of Germany's policy must be, as I have said, to lead the country from its position of dependence into that of a co-operating nation with equal rights in the community of free peoples. The path which has led us nearer to this aim has been steep and stony. Consider, for example, the debate in this House on the Petersberg agreement which relieved us of a number of particularly onerous restrictions from the Potsdam era. That agreement, too, had to be ratified against Social-Democrat opposition.

Not long after this we were asked if we would join the Council of Europe, the first joint organization of the free and democratic peoples of Europe. We were invited by those with whom five years previously our only relations had been armed combat. We accepted – once again in the face of Social-Democrat opposition. If the Council of Europe had been merely a forum of European public opinion in which for the first time again representatives of the European countries could come together and discuss questions in a comradely spirit it would still have been worth while to join. But out of this first meeting in the Council of Europe developed the discussion of the plan that the French Foreign Minister of the day, Robert Schuman, had worked out in a truly European spirit. At the time his plan was laughed at as utopian, and it was opposed by those who could not, or would not, understand it. The agreement which led to the establishment of the European Coal and Steel Community was

C

subsequently ratified by this House – once again in the face of Social-Democrat opposition.

The realization that we must continue along this path of European co-operation, and the feeling that we were all faced by the same danger, led to the conclusion of the agreement for European Defence which this House is now called upon to ratify today. This agreement has been concluded not only by the six countries which belong to the European Coal and Steel Community, but by special arrangement it has been joined by Great Britain and the United States. We shall adopt this agreement in its third reading today – once again, I fear, against the opposition of the Social Democrats.

A growing recognition of the common fate of all the countries of Europe led to the six Foreign Ministers anticipating Article 38 of the agreement on September 10th 1952 by instructing the special meeting in Strasbourg to work out a draft European Defence Community. The Strasbourg meeting agreed to do this – once again in spite of Social-Democrat opposition – and at the beginning of March the Statutes Committee concluded its work. It put forward a draft agreement drawn up by the politically responsible representatives of the six countries concerned, and the Strasbourg meeting adopted it by fifty votes, with five abstentions. From the beginning the representatives of those countries which were not for the time being taking part in this act of integration worked actively both in the Statutes Committee and in the full meeting; and through their mouthpieces, and with the support of all political parties, they expressed their full approval of the draft and of the truly European solution it proposed. The only absentees were, once again, the Social-Democrat opposition.

Allow me to recall briefly how this draft agreement came into being. The Special Meeting constituted itself on September 15th, and the Statutes Committee began its work a few days later. By January 7th the special meeting in Strasbourg had accepted the principles placed before it, and on March 6th the second reading of the agreement began, and ended on March 10th the exact day laid down in the September 10th decision.

Let me quote from the report the committee laid before the special meeting in order to show you the spirit in which the work was carried on, and will, I hope, be carried on in the future:

'As after the First World War, but with incomparably stronger power, the idea of Europe arouses the hopes of all peoples and influences the actions of European Governments. It is no longer a political ideal but a vital necessity. Those peoples who live on the plains of Europe will be able to survive only if they band together, for since the last war the composition of the world has been alarmingly simplified. The political catastrophes of recent years have awakened a feeling of solidarity amongst the peoples of Europe and a realization that solidarity is a matter of life and death. Europe is increasingly feeling the need to organize itself, to unite, and to create a common market, since without it the individual economies would be doomed to stagnation and finally disaster.'

And again:

'This European community, whose principles are laid down in these statutes, will be neither a federation of States nor a federal State. It unites the most varied forms of the classic State. At the same time it differs very clearly and definitely from a coalition or alliance resting solely on international agreements or arrangements. Such constructions allow all antagonisms to remain in being, and they are dominated by the principle of hegemony. In a community such as the draft proposes the specific ways of life of the peoples that make up the community will be guaranteed. The hegemony of any individual State, or any group of States, within the Community is out of the question.'

It has been suggested that we are on a bad path which can lead only to a 'Little Europe', but this objection is no longer valid. First of all, such an agreement is possible only with parties prepared to accept it; and, secondly, to bring 155 million people together in the heart of Europe can hardly be regarded as a small matter. Finally, I should like to point out that when this community comes into being – and I feel confident that it will – its intention will never be to exclude any other European state or nation. This is a point we have always stressed in our dealings with the representatives of Great Britain and the Scandinavian states. It should also not be forgotten that it has been founded with the full approval, and, indeed, support of those who, for reasons which do not directly concern us, feel that they cannot yet play a positive part in such an integration.

In this respect I should like to quote two of many similar

67

statements. One was made by a Conservative Member of the British Parliament, Mr Longden, and it is particularly interesting because it confirms almost textually what a British Labour MP, Mr Robens,* also said:

'We are all living through a historical epoch, perhaps a turning point in world history. We hold the key to security and prosperity in our hands. But I am afraid that unless Europe does not soon make a move to organize itself into federations or confederations, the United States and Great Britain will lose confidence in it and withdraw into isolation. Let us hope that such a misfortune will not come about. I therefore welcome the work of the Constitution Committee, and I should like to express my sincere good wishes for its success. I feel that a good piece of work has been done, and I am confident that despite the political uncertainty which exists in some countries we will both be able to complete our work, and that an appropriate plan will be presented to all national parliaments as soon as possible. The fact is that we have no choice. Europe must awaken and close its ranks or fall apart and perish.'

Does this sound as though our intentions were directed in any way against Britain? The Danish Social Democratic Deputy, Jacobsen, referring to the same draft, said:

'As a European I feel impelled to express my admiration at the courage and the freedom from prejudice with which the six countries are going forward into a new era. Go just as far as you possibly can, I say. Set us all an example! One day, it is to be hoped, we shall all follow you.'

Can anyone really say seriously after this that such a European Community as we have in mind is directed in any way against the Scandinavian countries and should therefore be dropped?

A common understanding binds all the agreements I have mentioned. The countries of Europe have to choose whether they will come together to save themselves by their joint efforts, or whether they will allow themselves to be balkanized in self-chosen isolation, and ultimately be drawn into the ranks of the satellite States to perish. My political friends and I prefer the former alternative, which is the only way to turn the enemies of yesterday into the partners of today and the friends of tomorrow. It is the only way to restore lost

*Now Lord Robens.

confidence and bring the countries of Europe into a joint community. Only in this way can we ever hope to settle our economic, political and – if the need arises – military problems together and for each other, and never against each other.

It has been objected here that this agreement does not immediately restore Germany's full sovereignty, that there are dangers involved in its provisions, and that, quite generally, the conclusion of these various agreements must hamper our efforts to secure the reunification of our country. At this point perhaps we should ask ourselves what sovereignty really is. The almost superstitious idea of national omnipotence and independence which arose in Europe – often as the result of rival power politics – belongs to a distorted and degenerate conception of a narrow-minded nationalism such as was used again and again to justify and cover up abuses of proper and legitimate power. I do not accept such false ideas of national sovereignty. In our Constitution we have already declared ourselves ready and willing to transfer some part of our national sovereignty to a new joint supra-national order to the same extent, and at the same time, as other States are prepared to do. We have not changed our minds on this point, and what still remains to us is a true and undistorted national consciousness.

I want Germans to be allowed to decide specifically German questions for themselves without outside interference, and this is precisely the sense of the agreement which now takes the place of the Occupation Statute. I am certainly not in favour of any backstairs methods to secure the right to take decisions, under the cloak of the alleged interests of the German people, which would, in fact, really be against their interests. Indeed, I am firmly convinced that anything calculated to disturb the peace between the free and democratic peoples would be against the true interests of the German people, because the future of the free peoples is the vital interest of them all.

The second objection refers to the so-called provisos. Now I, too, should be happy if provisos were no longer necessary, but we must remember that they arise out of the given situation. Or, to put it quite bluntly, they are the result of our collapse, which has had far-reaching consequences for our own inner structure, and has conjured up new dangers for the whole world.

The first proviso refers to Berlin, and it is the inevitable result of the tragic situation of that city, thanks to the deplorable Potsdam agreement. We should not forget, however, that Appendix A to the agreement recognizes the special role Berlin has played in the defence of the free world. It underlines the solidarity of the Federal Republic with Berlin, and identifies the fate and the security of Berlin with the fate and security of the Federal Republic. At the same time, this security is identical with that of all those who ratify the agreement and associate themselves with it. In my view the mention of Berlin in this connection is a proper expression of the thanks and appreciation we all owe to the very gallant inhabitants of that city.

The proviso referring to the reunification of Germany is surely a logical consequence of a fact that none of us can deny: namely, that we cannot bring about reunification on our own but only together with those who bear the responsibility for the present separation.

The so-called emergency proviso, which has been reduced to a minimum by the built-in guarantees, seems to me an inevitable consequence of the fact that Allied troops are still on German soil; and, in my opinion, should still be on German soil, in order to co-operate with us in the defence of our land and freedom. Prominent German politicians have demanded that at least sixty American divisions should be stationed here in order to defend us. Can anyone seriously suppose that foreign troops would consent to remain on German soil to defend what are primarily German interests if we refused them the right to defend themselves in circumstances where it might prove impossible for us to guarantee the maintenance of order? If we want to refuse them that right then at least we must be logical and say that we do not want them on our soil at all. Thank goodness, only a minority of the Federal Landtag, which is fortunately not present, has suggested anything of the sort.

Let me now deal with the one objection which is of real political importance: namely, that this agreement must hamper, and even prevent, the reunification of Germany within the framework of a free and democratic order. Incidentally, I should regard it as unworthy to enter into any discussions as to which side takes this vital question more to heart. It is neither chauvinism nor exaggerated nationalism when I say that there is no decent German who is not constantly troubled by this problem, and who does not desire from the bottom of his heart that the great powers should end the present state of affairs. We Germans have the right to demand this precisely because we are in favour of a European community, because we want freedom and peace. The wretched zonal lines of demarcation not only carve up our Fatherland, but they carve up Europe itself. There are

70

eighteen million Europeans who belong to the German race now living in anxiety, distress and slavery on the other side of those lines. It is therefore the task of all the free peoples of the world to resolve this problem, because as long as there are people living without freedom the principle of freedom cannot be said to be established. So long as millions of people live without peace in their lives the peace of the world is endangered. And so long as millions of people want to join us in advocating a European community but are prevented from doing so by brutal terror, there will remain a running sore in Europe.

A recognition of this truly European problem has guided the policy of the Federal Government. It is precisely for this reason that we stand by those agreements whose preamble declares that they were concluded 'in the recognition that the re-establishment of a completely free and united Germany by peaceable means, and the attainment of a freely agreed solution on the basis of a treaty of peace, is a joint and fundamental objective of all the signatory States'.

We know that the millions of people in the Soviet zone expect us to continue along this path because the defence of our freedom is the condition of their liberation. Our partners, those who acknowledge the reunification of Germany as their aim too, thereby undertake joint responsibility for the millions of people in the Soviet zone. Our signature under the agreement is not only for the Federal Republic but for all the sixty-six million people on both sides of the zonal frontier, and it makes them share in the fate of all the free peoples of the world.

I should like to give a clear and definite answer to all those abroad who, whether from folly or ill-will, doubt our intentions: we do not want war, and we are prepared to go to the limit and make the greatest possible sacrifices in order to avoid it. Only a dangerous lunatic can possibly believe that the unification of Germany could be brought about as the result of a bloody clash between East and West. Germany knows more about the horrors of war than any other country in the world. She does not wish to become the cockpit – and the graveyard – of a Third World War.

Therefore we shall go on demanding that a Four-Power Conference should meet to settle the German question. But such a conference must have only one point on its agenda: the re-establishment of a united Germany on the basis of a free and democratic order, free in her decisions in so far as they serve the German people and the community of free peoples and bode no harm to others.

There are only a few poor fools and a few despicable yes-men who do not know, or pretend not to know, who stands in the way of a solution, who terrorizes eighteen million people in the Soviet zone and refuses them the right of self-determination. The events of the past few months have been sufficient to open all eyes, and when we discuss these agreements we should think of the millions of people in the Soviet zone who remain Germans on German soil despite the terror, whilst hoping and waiting for a joint future with us; and also those many thousands who have fled to the West because they could no longer stand their slavery, because in their anxiety they preferred to sacrifice everything they possessed there to flee here to an uncertain and difficult future.

The fools and the yes-men deny this dangerous threat to human liberty, to the democratic order, and those inalienable values I uphold both as a German and a Christian. Happily – and here I should like to underline what the Federal Chancellor said on this subject – there is no difference of opinion between the great German democratic parties concerning the ultimate objective. As the Chancellor pointed out, they are all well aware of their joint responsibility, and they all clearly realize that any threat must be met with concerted resistance. I should like to refer to what I assume was an officious article by Colleague Luetkens in yesterday's issue of *Aussenpolitik*, and quote one sentence from it in order to clear up certain ambiguities which have arisen in German minds. Writing on behalf of the Social Democratic Party, our colleague Luetkens declared:

'In the view of all the big parties in Germany the Federal Government should make a military contribution to our security.'

We are thus all in agreement on this first step. I also think I am right in saying that we are all agreed that any threat of danger should be faced jointly, since we are simply not in a position to take effective action on our own. It would seem, too, that we are also in complete agreement that Germany must unquestionably take the side of the free peoples of the world, and work together with them.

Thus we are in fundamental agreement on our aim. The only differences between us are with regard to ways and means. Now the Federal Government has mapped out a very clear path, and the agreements I have mentioned represent stages along it. So far this path has undeniably proved the correct one, but up till now the Opposition has always opposed it. I therefore say again here that the Federal Landtag and the whole German people – indeed, the whole world – have a right to know not only what the Social Democratic Party is against, but also what it is for. If the Opposition really has nothing better to suggest, would it be unfair to say: if we are in agreement as to our ultimate aim – and it would appear that we are – wouldn't it be good democracy to allow the majority to decide what steps must be taken to reach this jointly agreed aim?

I have already made it quite clear that for our part we are quite determined to go on along this path, and we want a continuation of the policy of the Federal Government. Naturally, we are not unmindful of the fact that we shall meet all sorts of difficulties on the way. For one thing, deep-rooted resentments still exist everywhere. That mistrust which has poisoned the relations between peoples in the past, and has frequently made peaceable existence together impossible, has not yet entirely disappeared from the world. There are still a whole series of outstanding questions which are as yet unresolved. Let me mention just a few of varying degrees of importance as an example of what I expect and hope for from the carrying out of these agreements, and from a spirit of real European co-operation.

First of all there is the Saar. Franco-German relations are still being disturbed by this problem; nevertheless I hope it will prove possible to lift it out of the unfortunate atmosphere of prestige politics. The Saar is inhabited by Germans, whilst France has economic interests in the area. With good will on both sides it should be possible to come to a satisfactory arrangement. But the worst possible thing would be to try to turn the Saar into a new State, or into anything resembling a State. We are working to form a European community, to tear down customs barriers and abolish political frontiers, to co-ordinate the policy of all members of the European community in all spheres, and finally to grow together into a federation or confederation. So how could we possibly tolerate the setting up of a new political entity with political frontiers in the heart of Europe, particularly when any such construction most obviously lacks any political or historical justification and runs counter to plain common sense. I think we have found a good transitional solution in the European constitutional committee, and I can only hope that the governments concerned will let themselves be guided by the same idea when they negotiate with each other.

I should like to utter a word of warning to our friends in the West, and particularly in France. In France and Germany – indeed, in all other countries – people realize very clearly that Franco-German relationships are the key problem of European politics, and are likely to remain so. Both sides are burdened with a heritage of mistrust and mutual fear, and I fully realize that it will take a long time before we are rid of it. But I can say for myself and my political friends, and I think for the overwhelming majority of the German people: we are determined to do all we can to establish a relationship of true and solid friendship between our two great peoples. We ask our neighbours in the West, and particularly in France, to give us their confidence, and approach Europe's great problem in the same spirit.

There are still one or two other outstanding questions, some of which were touched on during the second reading. I should like in particular to ask the Federal Government to negotiate for the settlement of the question of German property abroad, where this has not already been done, the protection of German trade-marks, and other economic matters. I should also like it to be made clear – and I think it will be – that these new negotiations should not take place as between victors and vanquished, but as between partners, and in a spirit of partnership.

There are thousands of people, displaced persons, in Germany who are still waiting in the hope that they and their property shall no longer be subject to the arbitrary decisions of local officers, but will be treated in that spirit of partnership and friendship which alone can give these agreements their real significance.

The same is true of the frontier problems. Take the situation on the Dutch border. It is not a political question of very great international importance, but it is vital for those directly concerned. Now I feel that this problem should not be approached in the spirit of 1945, but in a way that will show all concerned that we are again living in a truly European community.

Our recent debate raised the question of those Germans who have been sentenced by Allied courts. Now I really do not think that anyone will suspect me of favouring criminal elements when I say that in many cases individual Germans could just find no way out of the conflict between duty and humanity. A very great deal has, in fact, already been done to mitigate extreme harshness – more than German public opinion is aware of – and I now welcome the news I have just received according to which the American Government has decided not to wait for the ratification of the agreements and for the establishment of the Board of Review provided for in them, but will make a start with the review of individual cases at once in order, wherever possible, to grant a pardon, and thus put an end to a situation no one wishes to pursue any further. I think this evidence of good will is sufficient indication of how important these agreements are, even though they have not yet been ratified. You can see that the spirit in which they were concluded is already at work.

As I have already pointed out, the reasons which persuaded us to vote in favour of the second reading have in the meantime, we feel, become even stronger. As far as we are concerned our aim in accepting these agreements is to enter into a community of free peoples as an equal partner, and at the same time to gain friends ready to share our fate with us. These agreements will enable us to break out once and for all from an isolation forced on us by the wretched past. They will gain us the support not only of the five other countries which are members of the European Coal and Steel Community and of the Defence Community, but also of Britain and the United States, whose governments have signed the supplementary agreements. These agreements also represent a further step forward towards the United Europe we all desire. Six countries in the heart of Europe have already made up their minds, and eventually other countries will join with them. Finally, the agreements will reinforce the well-being and social security not only of our own people, but of all others, and at the same time free us from the crippling chains of economic autarky and sterile self-sufficiency. We say 'yes' to these agreements because from the bottom of our hearts we want to see a free and independent Germany co-operating in the peaceable building up of the world and not excluded from it, because we are in favour of peace and realize that we cannot preserve it on our own, because we want a united Germany once more and realize that we need friends to help us attain it, because we are in favour of freedom and know that it will be destroyed unless those who love freedom come together to defend it, and because we are good Europeans and know that these agreements will prove strong pillars of a European community. We say 'yes' to these agreements without reserve, without qualification and without mistrust, because we are convinced that on the day the others say 'yes' too, and, above all, when we are brought together not by our economic or military interests, but by a joint recognition that our future lies together, a new epoch will open up for all our countries and for Europe itself.

# 8

# Free Elections in both Parts of Germany*

SINCE it came into existence the Government of the German Federal Republic has, with the approval of the overwhelming majority of parliament, repeatedly declared that the division of Germany is one of the main causes for the disturbance of European order and therefore a threat to world peace. The Federal Government therefore holds that the reunification of Germany is an urgent necessity. The most important step on the way to this desirable reunification is the holding of free elections in the Federal Republic, in the Soviet Zone, and in Berlin.

The Federal Government and the overwhelming majority of the Federal Landtag feel that free elections will be possible only when the necessary conditions are established throughout the whole electoral area. Free elections can take place only when conditions everywhere throughout the electoral area allow each inhabitant to cast his vote freely, in full possession of his civic rights of liberty and equality.

For this reason the Federal Government has, with the support of all the parties in the Federal Landtag – with the one exception of the Communist Party, which enjoys the support of less than four per cent of the total electorate – asked the United Nations to appoint a commission of investigation to decide whether existing conditions in the Federal Republic and also in Berlin and in the Soviet Zone are such as to allow the holding of really free elections. The Federal Government would welcome the speedy appointment of such a commission, and would certainly give it every possible facility to

*Speech delivered on December 8th 1951 in support of a proposal for the appointment of a UNO commission to examine the possibility of free elections in both parts of Germany.

77

investigate constitutional conditions in the Federal Republic. After the collapse, both the Federal Republic and the Soviet Zone adopted constitutions, in each case with the approval of the appropriate occupation authorities. Ostensibly both these constitutions provide for the establishment of a democratic order in the territories concerned. The Preamble of the Constitution of the Federal Republic declares that those Germans who adopted it did so also in the name of all their fellow Germans who were prevented by conditions from co-operating.

Its concluding passage declares: 'The appeal still remains to the whole of the German people to complete the unity and freedom of Germany in free self-determination.'

In this sense the German people on both sides of the zonal frontier feel themselves as united today as ever in the past. And in this spirit the Federal Government has always felt itself responsible for all Germans, no matter on what side of the border they live. In the same spirit the following report on civil liberty in Germany attempts to see the country as a unity, but it also shows to what extent this unity is endangered and disrupted by the discrepancy between the conditions under which Germans live on this side of the border and the other. The discrepancy cannot be recognized from a textual comparison of the Constitution of the Federal Republic with that of the so-called German Democratic Republic. In fact, whoever reads the text of the latter might well conclude that a society based on normal law and order also exists in that part of Germany which is under communist control. The basic rights and liberties of the citizen are all there – on paper, but only on paper; they are not a political reality. Therefore anyone wishing to establish just what the political reality is must ignore the formal text of the constitution and see how the population really lives.

Not only the Constitution itself but the constitutional structure in the Federal Republic guarantees all citizens the full exercise of all their civic rights in complete freedom. The Constitution guarantees freedom of conscience and speech, the right to organize, and the right to personal freedom. And all these rights are reinforced in law and practice. All institutions which can form public opinion, such as newspapers, wireless, the schools and churches, are free to pursue their activities as they think fit. The right to form political parties is also fully established. And all these civic rights are protected by independent courts. The lawful order which guarantees these liberties in the Federal Republic is not merely written into the Constitution, but political practice is fully in accordance with all the requirements of a lawful democratic order. The Federal Government would therefore welcome the appointment of a United Nations Commission of inquiry into the operation of these democratic principles in all spheres of public life and in all parts of the Federal Republic.

In the Soviet Zone, on the other hand, there is an increasing divergence between formal constitutional liberties and actual political practice. Since the formation of the so-called Socialist Unity Party all other parties and all other free organizations have been systematically suppressed. The suggestion that a multi-party system exists there is just not true. The fact is that the democratic parties which were formed there in 1945 have since been steadily deprived of their elected organs and degraded to more or less dependent parts of the dominant Socialist Unity Party. For example, the Christian Democratic Union reconstituted itself in the autumn of 1947 at a congress with democratically elected representatives from all over the Soviet Zone. But as soon as it became the mouthpiece of the opposition it was deprived of its leaders. From my own experience I can tell you of a conference in Berlin in 1947 at which a thousand delegates of the Christian Democratic Union were present. Within a very few weeks the united demonstrated will of this party had been completely nullified. In discussions at which I was present together with representatives of the Soviet forces of occupation, it was announced that the democratically elected chairman of the party could no longer be regarded as its political representative. Protests that such action on the part of the Soviet authorities violated all democratic principles were just ignored. The only representatives of the Christian Democratic Union left in office were those the Soviet occupation authorities and the Socialist Unity Party were prepared to approve. All the others were removed from their posts either by ukase of the Soviet occupation authorities or by the action of local groups of the Socialist Unity Party – to the accompaniment of 'spontaneous' but actually carefully organized demonstrations. You must allow me to refrain from mentioning any names in this connection, since to do so would be to endanger people still living on the other side of the border. Exactly the same thing happened to the Liberal Democratic Party, and to this we have a witness present here in the person of my colleague Doctor Schäfer, our Vice-President. The fate of the Social Democratic Party in the Soviet Zone is further proof of the complete

79

dictatorship of the Socialist Unity Party. Formally there are still several political parties in the Soviet Zone, but, in fact, they are nothing but dependent auxiliaries of the Socialist Unity Party. Those representatives of the real democratic parties who opposed this development had to make their escape to Berlin or to the Federal Republic, or risk arrest and imprisonment.

The thoroughness with which the Christian Democratic Union has been emasculated can be seen from a passage in the so-called *Twenty-two Theses of Christian Realism* the CDU congress was forced to adopt last October:

> The movement founded by Karl Marx, which finds its most logical development in the Soviet Union, serves us as an example in the fight for a new and better society, and we must therefore continue to co-operate with the supporters of Marxist-Leninism.

This sort of thing could be quoted *ad nauseam* to show the subjection of all other so-called political parties to the ruling Socialist Unity Party. It was not until this situation had been brought about that the authorities in the Soviet Zone dared to hold a general election in the Zone. It took place on October 15th 1950, and the only parties, groups and organizations allowed to take any part were those firmly in the grip of the Socialist Unity Party. Even so, there were no candidates representing different parties, and the electors were presented with single lists of names approved by the occupation authorities. The distribution of the seats amongst these candidates was arranged in advance. The whole procedure can therefore hardly be termed an election in any real sense of the term. It was no more than the gerrymandered approval of a previously arranged result. All the voter could do was to accept or reject the list as it stood. No free discussion took place before the elections and there was no opportunity of selecting the candidates. And when the so-called election actually took place, the territorial and factory representatives of the Socialist Unity Party, and the officials in charge of the polling stations, often insisted that the voting should be open, so that it was even made impossible for the electors to reject the whole list, as they were formally entitled to, because anyone who might have felt inclined to vote 'No' was well aware from past experience what would happen to him if he did and it became known. Life under two dictatorships had at least taught him that. In addition, the official election propaganda on the day was conducted in such a fashion that everyone was made to understand that if he stayed away from the voting there would subsequently be trouble for him with the local authorities. Those of us who have lived under a totalitarian system know only too well all the tricks by which apparently free elections can be turned into a grim farce. There is no sense in any election which does not give voters at least two clear choices. There can be no true voting if there is only one list of candidates. And when the electors are compelled to vote by moral intimidation and physical force there can be no abstentions either. And, finally, if the ballot is not secret then even he who would vote 'No' if he were allowed to follow his inner convictions has to vote 'Yes' instead. Naturally, such systematic violations of the principle of the free, secret and democratic vote produced the desired result, and according to official Soviet reports 98·5 per cent of the electorate went to the polls, and 12,097,105 voted for the 'Unity' list. 34,060 brave souls are said to have voted against it. These grotesque figures are in themselves ample proof of the dishonesty of the whole proceeding.

There is no legal possibility of an opposition in the Soviet Zone. In the same way there can be no opposition within the parties either, because the political activity of each member is carefully controlled, and each party member knows that absence from a meeting or demonstration can affect his livelihood. And as for resigning from the party – he knows that it would immediately be reported to the Security Service.

At the same time the Soviet Zone Constitution guarantees the personal freedom of the citizen, the inviolability of his home, his right to live where he pleases, and his right to express his views openly. Formally speaking, no one can be penalized for exercising any of these rights, but, in fact, in the Soviet Zone there is a Security Service reminiscent of the Gestapo, with 150 centres and 4,500 officials. In addition there is an army of spies estimated at fifty thousand. This Security Service needs no warrant for arrests, and in particular it carefully checks all contacts between citizens of the Soviet Zone and the outside world – so carefully that when a man is brought up on a political charge he is almost invariably presented with photostat copies of his correspondence with friends and relatives in the Federal Republic. Any citizen of the Soviet Zone who took his formal right to free speech seriously would soon find himself in prison, and innumerable cases could be quoted in which this has happened. The citizens of the Soviet Zone have no protection against arbitrary persecution, because the executive is not that of a democratic régime, but the dictatorial Socialist Unity Party. Listen to the report of the Central Committee of that party to its third congress. Referring to local mayors, i.e., to the representatives of municipal government, in so far as one can speak of any such thing in the Soviet Zone, the report says:

'It is the duty of Mayors and other municipal officials to take a more active part in the factory-council work of the Party, and, in particular, to support its educational work.'

There is no protection whatever against arbitrary administrative measures. In the Federal Republic, on the other hand, the judiciary is completely independent of political influence. No one may be deprived of his right to be tried by a judge. Exceptional courts do not exist, and no one can be arrested without a warrant issued by a magistrate. There are no concentration camps or any similar institutions. None of these essential conditions for a free life exists in the Soviet Zone. Perhaps the most extreme example of this sort of thing in the Soviet Zone is the position of judges. In the official report of the Third Congress of the Socialist Unity Party I have already mentioned, the Central Committee describes the task of a judge in the Soviet Zone as follows:

'The aim of democratic jurisprudence is to reinforce the authority of the State and eliminate its enemies. In this respect our People's Judges and People's Prosecutors have shown themselves fully worthy of their tasks.'

*Neue Justiz*, the official law publication, is even franker:

'The court is the organ of the Dictatorship of the Proletariat, and its purpose is to protect the interests of the toiling masses under the leadership of the working class, and it is therefore a socialist-type court. In consequence it is fundamentally different from a bourgeois court. Its object is to contribute to the tasks of social and cultural construction, to help lay the foundations of a socialist economy, and to suppress capitalist elements.'

To make sure that the judiciary of the Soviet Zone thoroughly carries out this mission in the interests of the Socialist Unity Party, most of the trained professional judges have been dismissed, and 'People's Judges' and 'People's Prosecutors' have been appointed in their stead. These are Party officials hurriedly trained in special short-term courses. The latest official figures show that 721 out of 1,169 judges are now so-called 'People's Judges', and 291 out of 351 prosecutors are so-called 'People's Prosecutors'. It is also not surprising to hear that 93 per cent of all prosecutors and 65 per cent of all judges are members of the Socialist Unity Party. According to information I have just received, the last professional trained jurist in Land Brandenburg has just been relieved of his post. In 1945 there were about three thousand lawyers in the Soviet Zone. Today there are only 941 still practising. From January 1st 1949 to June 1951 158 lawyers fled from the Soviet Zone into the Federal Republic. A full description of the state of jurisprudence in the Soviet Zone would fill volumes, but in this report I can give only a few figures. We know, for example, that 40,800 people are under arrest there for what can only be termed political offences. 24,800 of them are political prisoners pure and simple. 8,000 are so-called economic criminals. A further 8,000 are being held by the security services. From April to June 1950 3,500 political offenders were sentenced to long terms of imprisonment in Waldheim in Saxony. Over 3,000 of them were innocent men in the eyes of the law. In the period from January 1st 1951 to May 15th 1951 6,425 young people were sentenced by Soviet Zone courts for political offences. Eighteen students and one adult, whose offence was that they had prepared and distributed leaflets during the elections in October, were sentenced to a total of 130 years hard labour. In this connection a decree issued by the Minister of Justice in the Soviet Zone on September 5th 1951 is interesting:

'Whoever attacks our anti-fascist democratic order, whoever disturbs the building up of our peace economy, commits a punishable offence and will be called to account for his criminal activities. Prisoners of this kind are therefore not political offenders but common criminals, and it is hereby forbidden to refer to them as 'political prisoners'.'

In these circumstances the concentration camps in the Soviet Zone could well be replaced by prisons. There were at least 185,000 people in these camps. 96,000 died in the camps, 37,000 were deported to Soviet territory proper, and about 14,500 were transferred to prison.

Political rights and personal liberty are also nullified in the Soviet Zone by the system of forced labour and deportation. Everyone is registered at the labour centres, and at any time anyone, irrespective of where he lives, his family circumstances, or his previous training, can be sent to forced labour. For example, 200,000 of the 250,000 workers in the uranium mines, and so on, are such forced labourers, and amongst them are 25,000 women and young girls. By Ministry of Labour regulations women, even mothers with small children, can be denied relief if they refuse to accept work allotted to them. There is no protection whatever against such arbitrary measures. In flagrant contradiction to the written Constitution, there is no right to organize, no right to strike, and no right to live in any particular place. The so-called Free German Labour Federation is, like the Socialist Unity Party, not an organization to defend the interests of working people, but a government instrument to oppress them. The ordinary citizen in the Soviet Zone is rendered even more defenceless by the subjugation of the press to the official propaganda apparatus. In its report to the Third Congress of the Socialist Unity Party, the Central Committee describes the tasks of the press as follows:

'The press assists in the struggle against the anti-party elements within the Party, and against the camouflaged and open enemies of the Republic in the ranks of the bourgeois parties and elsewhere in the Republic.'

Newspapers and so on from the Federal Republic and from other democratic countries are not formally prohibited in the Soviet Zone, but anyone attempting to circulate them can be certain of severe punishment.

But perhaps you are wondering what the source of all this information is? From January 1st 1950 to September 30th 1951 no less than 322,254 people fled from the Soviet Zone to West Berlin and the Federal Republic. All these fugitives abandoned their homes and their jobs and everything they possessed to find freedom with us. They are all living witnesses to what I have said, and they are all available to give evidence before the United Nations Commission of Inquiry we have asked for. The reunification of the four zones of occupation and Berlin can be brought about only by a free decision of the whole German people. No one can relieve us of our obligation in this matter. Discussions between representatives of the Federal Republic and the Soviet zonal administration could achieve nothing. Our opposite numbers in any such discussion would be the very people who are responsible for the suppression of freedom in the

Soviet Zone. Further, they have no right or authority to speak on behalf of the eighteen million Germans in that zone, since they have no democratic mandate. At any time within recent years they could have reintroduced democratic freedom into their zone if they had wanted to. We therefore do not feel that an inquiry conducted by representatives of the four zones of occupation would meet the requirements put forward by the German Federal Government and the Federal Landtag. The state of affairs I have described to you is unquestionably the tragic result of the division of Germany into four zones. The occupation authority in the Eastern Zone is responsible for its administration. Instead of establishing a democratic order based on the rights of man it has allowed a small group of men to set up an administration based on force and fraud, thus robbing millions of Germans of their freedom and forcing them to live in constant fear of political reprisals. That is why the Federal Government and the Federal Landtag have called for an independent inquiry along the lines suggested in their declaration of September 27th 1951. In the name of the Federal Government and of the overwhelming majority of the Federal Landtag I can only say that we have nothing to fear from such an inquiry. Indeed, we should welcome it. All departments of the Federal Government and of the Länder, all democratic parties, all organizations, and all institutions forming public opinion, such as the press and the wireless, would gladly provide such an independent commission of inquiry with a full insight into internal political relations and conditions generally in the territory of the Federal Republic. Our insistence that such a commission should be independent is, unfortunately, a necessary guarantee that its investigations would be conducted with complete objectivity and in a spirit of peaceable mediation. On our part we should see no interference with the rights of the German people in the appointment of such a commission. Indeed, we should welcome it because we know that its unprejudiced report would assist us to attain that object in which we are all completely at one with the eighteen million Germans living in the Soviet Zone: namely, the re-establishment of German unity by peaceful means so that all Germans may enjoy the blessings of lasting peace and real freedom!

# 9

# The German Problem and a Joint Foreign Policy*

THE discussion which followed the excellent report of our colleague Benvenuti will once again draw the attention of the world to the Council of Europe. The Council performs the important task of analysing, criticizing and encouraging world political development. Perhaps its greatest achievement is that it has developed into a forum in which joint problems can be discussed in a spirit of mutual understanding and friendship, and that these discussions have increasingly persuaded all those who take part in them that the hopes of the European nations and the aims of their national policies are identical.

It is not so very long ago that European countries, or at least some of them, thought that what was good for others must necessarily be bad for them. In my view it is the historical achievement of the Council of Europe to have dismissed this false assumption, and to have contributed to a new and fruitful understanding amongst the European peoples that their political, economic and social developments are indissolubly connected; that what is good for any one country is good for all the others, and that a failure and set-back suffered by the one must burden and hamper all the others.

Only in this way is it to be explained that the advisory meeting and the Ministerial Council have organically extended their authority, and that the spirit of solidarity, mutual understanding and mutual obligation has developed and facilitated the solution of really big and decisive problems. I count myself fortunate that for years I have

*Speech delivered at the Advisory Meeting of the Council of Europe on April 18th 1956.

had the honour to take part in this work. The fact that I can go on doing so today from another angle I regard only as imposing an increased obligation.

It was here that President Robert Schuman announced his courageous plan for the formation of a European Coal and Steel Community. This was a decisive step on the way to European unity and on the way to Franco-German friendship, which is one of the essential preliminaries of such a policy. It was here that the first discussion on the necessity of jointly opposing any threat to our joint security and freedom took place. It was here that the basic principles of the European Defence Community were worked out and subsequently found their expression in Western European Union, even if in a different form from that at first envisaged. This body has discussed the great task of European Political unity, and approved the idea which is now being carried forward – if once again in a changed form – following on the Messina decisions. I gladly associate myself with the remarks of the previous speaker, M. Pineau, who stressed the importance of this work, and I assure you that the German Federal Government is anxious to do all it can to carry out these decisions, and in such a way that the number of countries taking part should not be restricted.

Last autumn the Advisory Meeting discussed the excellent report of our colleague M. de Menthon. The resolution adopted at the time expressed the hopes and expectations of the people represented. I feel that the resolution reflected the longing of all European and non-European peoples for peace in a particularly happy and persuasive way, when it expressed the hope that the conference of Foreign Ministers in Geneva would bring about a real relaxation of tension. Pointing out that the arms race was a tragic but inevitable consequence of mistrust and tension in the world, Resolution 87 added the wish that the Disarmament Committee of the United Nations might successfully continue its efforts. At the same time the meeting did not close its eyes to the harsh facts of the situation, and it uttered a timely warning against the inadequate and dangerous character of any agreement with the Soviet Union on European security unless it embraced the reunification of Germany. At the same time it indicated the way to a solution when it stressed the logical connection between the denial of independence and freedom to a great number of European peoples on the one hand, and the urgent necessity of restoring free and democratic conditions by holding free elections on the other. This resolution has lost nothing of its validity in the meantime.

In his report our colleague Benvenuti has set out to continue the discussion started then, and to give us an analysis of the world-political situation now facing us. On behalf of the Federal Government I should like to express my satisfaction both with the report and its presentation.

Unfortunately, the conference of Foreign Ministers in Geneva did not justify the hopes placed in it. The Foreign Ministers of France, the United Kingdom and the United States jointly submitted a memorandum with practical and far-reaching proposals calculated to meet the security requirements of all peoples and at the same time give the German people their freedom once more both at home and abroad. We greatly regret that the Soviet Foreign Minister was not even prepared to discuss these proposals seriously. The way in which he attempted to dismiss the essential connection between the German question and the security problem was a profound disappointment for us and for all those who wish to put an end to this intolerable state of tension. Very properly the Advisory Meeting put forward a demand for free elections in the clear recognition that those who do not acknowledge this elementary right of a free people are thereby violating the principle of self-determination and seeking to perpetuate a state of injustice which increases international tension and endangers the peace of the world.

I need do no more than underline the observations of the Reporter on Soviet ideas of security, but I must add that I reproach the Soviet Union because its attitude has frustrated our efforts to bring about a relaxation of tension, and denied the legitimate requirements of all peoples – not only of the German people – in this matter of security.

It has been claimed that a stable peace presupposes the creation of a so-called 'balance of power', whilst the Geneva proposals were calculated in the last resort to stabilize the real or supposed dominance of the two 'rival power groups'. The charge strikes me as both baseless and unjust.

It strikes me as wrong and dangerous to compare the interests and the aims of the two groups in this way, because in fact incommensurable quantities stand opposed to each other here. The Soviet Union still aims at world revolution, and makes no attempt to deny it. Its policy is expansive and aggressive. On the other hand, the attitude of the free world merely expresses its anxiety in face of a threat to its domestic and foreign security. To give this up, or even to allow it to be endangered, would be the first step, if not to subjugation then to voluntary surrender.

Six months have now passed since the second Geneva Conference, and since then surprising developments have taken place in the Soviet Union. Years after his death Stalin has been toppled from his throne. We are now hearing professions of loyalty to the idea of collective leadership, and there is even a suggestion that the Leninist dogma of the inevitability of war between Communism and the so-called capitalist world has been abandoned. In fact, the talk is now all about peaceful co-existence. However, the Twentieth Congress of the Communist Party of the Soviet Union provided us with a sobering interpretation of what is meant by peaceful co-existence as current Soviet political tactics.

I do not feel that we need venture into that jungle of ideological wrangling, particularly as the dialectics it involves are unfamiliar to us. It is enough if we recognize the plain facts, which have not changed. To topple a dead dictator, adopt a different phraseology, and – as we now hear – dissolve the Comintern, is not enough to persuade us that Soviet aims have changed. It is not so much that we are unwilling to believe that makes us suspicious because of past experience, but because it is our duty to remain watchful, and to demand deeds rather than words from them before we are convinced. So far such deeds have not been provided.

I should be very happy if I could honestly say that we are able to think differently, but, in fact, the Federal Government still feels that the political aims of the Soviet Union have not been changed. Perhaps they will change their propaganda and their tactics, as suggested by this new thesis of co-existence, and the efforts to show a different political face, but all the same we should be deceiving ourselves, perhaps dangerously, if in consequence we relaxed our efforts to defend freedom and security. What I am saying will not prevent us from following developments very closely and constantly re-analysing them, because the apparently greater elasticity of Soviet political leadership may offer new possibilities of solving the East–West problem, and the German problem embedded in it. Nevertheless, this new development may well contain new and perhaps even greater dangers, and they will be neither minimized nor disposed of by our refusing to see them. I hope that because I say this our colleague Pineau will not accuse me of lacking the will to conciliation and of being unduly pessimistic, or of allowing my words to be dictated by unjustifiable mistrust or fear.

The Federal Government and the Federal parliament have repeatedly stressed the indissoluble connection between the German problem and the problems of security and disarmament, and I am grateful for the support accorded by M. Theotokis here. I ask you to believe that what I have said here is certainly not intended to make disarmament and any relaxation of tension more difficult. No one can reproach a German for stressing the connection with the German problem, a question which we Germans find particularly painful because we feel ourselves under a political and moral obligation to the eighteen million of our fellow countrymen who live without freedom in the Soviet zone of occupation. On the other hand, do not suppose that in putting this matter into the foreground we are striving to secure special priority even for a justifiable national matter. We do it in the clear recognition that an answer must be found to this question before there can be any effective security system in Europe or any effectively controlled disarmament.

The Federal Government is the mouthpiece of the whole German people, but it does not say: we want neither security nor disarmament unless Germany is at the same time reunited. What it does say warningly is that an effective European security system, controlled disarmament and a relaxation of tension will prove impossible so long as a state of injustice is maintained in the heart of Europe, since that alone will create tension, and tension will prevent the atmosphere of confidence which is essential for any disarmament.

Let us take care not to regard security and disarmament as ideas that can be kept apart from each other. And we certainly don't want to regard them as antithetic. However, the Federal Government feels that no purely mechanical reduction of existing armaments will prove adequate. Germany wishes to be a partner in disarmament, but she can really fulfil her function of supporting security and peace only if she becomes a partner as *one* Germany. Only a united Germany can really give the requisite guarantees, and take an active part in the operation of effective controls.

Let no one doubt the solemn, indeed, the urgent, desire of the Federal Republic and of the whole German people to take the most active part in such a development. Let me remind you of Doctor Adenauer's declaration to the Federal parliament on May 27th last year. His contention that a real system of security can be based only on limited and controlled armaments still remains valid.

I do not wish to enter into a pointless discussion of whether there are priorities for the problems I have mentioned. The order may largely be determined by feelings, but the basis for the political decisions now before us must always be a joint recognition of their indissoluble relationship in practice. I am very glad that your Reporter Benvenuti underlined this so clearly and cogently. I therefore wholly approve of the supplement to the introductory report to Document Number 487. I feel it establishes a welcome and perhaps necessary connection with Resolution Number 87, which I also mentioned.

It is not our task to deal in any detail with the problem of disarmament here, and we may feel confident that the Commission of the United Nations will examine the complicated problem with the closest attention, but at least we may express the hope, and even the conviction, that the indissoluble connection between the problems I have mentioned will be just as clearly recognized in the disarmament negotiations as it has been in the discussions on the Western side which preceded the second Geneva Conference. I am to inform you that the Federal Government is also in favour of a limitation of armaments, and that it will always do its best to contribute to the carrying out of this great idea for peace. However, we should fail to recognize our task and fail to do our duty if we mistook illusions for hard facts. The aim of German policy – and here I know that I am speaking for the whole German people on both sides of the border – is to lead a free Germany as an equal partner into a community of free peoples based on peace and security.

# 10

## Problems of Germany's East European Policy*

WHEN I received the invitation to address you here I accepted with great pleasure, because I was very anxious to attend your gathering and be able to talk to you.

I bring you the greetings of the Federal Chancellor, who has asked me to express the warmest good wishes of the Federal Government for the success of your work and the well-being of you all. I am addressing you in full consciousness of the burden you have borne for a decade now: exile. You share this fate with millions of other people – not only from the other parts of East Germany, but from many other countries too – who have been robbed of their homes by dictatorship and war. Not that I think that to share such a fate is a consolation. However, it is important for you and for us to know that you are not alone in your troubles, and that we have to oppose injustice and mitigate suffering in many other parts of Europe, indeed, the world, in consequence of the great mass expulsions of our time.

Your homeland is one of thick forests, powerful rivers, gentle hills and ancient cities. The magic of this countryside speaks to us from the immortal verse of its greatest poet, Joseph von Eichendorff, who is also one of the masters of German lyricism. Your forefathers were the first, over five hundred years ago, to introduce the iron plough-share; they were the first to exploit your homeland's wealth of coal and ore, and create that other great centre of German mining and industry.

The men of Upper Silesia have outstanding achievements to their credit in all spheres of human activity. In addition to Joseph von

*Speech delivered at the Gathering of Upper Silesians in Bochum on July 1st 1956.

Eichendorff, there was also Gustav Freytag, who was born in Kreuzberg, and became one of the most prominent names in German literature of the last century. Many other famous names originated in Upper Silesia: Emin Pasha, the great explorer of Africa, whose real name was Eduard Schnitzer and who came from Oppeln; and Count Arco from Ratibor, one of the pioneers of radio. In our own days there is the chemist Kurt Alder of Königshütte, who was awarded the Nobel Prize in 1951. And how many people know that the brilliant architect of Cologne Cathedral, Ernst Friedrich Zwirner, was from Upper Silesia?

These are only a few of the great names that originated in your homeland, and are today a symbol of our all-German solidarity. In remembering them at the same time we honour the great services the whole people of Upper Silesia, the miners and the peasants, the pioneers and the builders, have rendered not only to Germany's economy and culture, but to those of Europe too.

We send our greetings to Upper Silesians wherever they may be, but in particular to those who have remained in their homes waiting and hoping for the Iron Curtain to rise and reunite those who are separated.

Quite a short glance at history is enough to show that such a peaceable reunification has nothing in common with nationalistic arrogance, but is, in fact, a just demand of the German people – indeed, of all peoples who believe that without freedom and justice there can be no lasting peace.

Your homeland on both sides of the Oder first entered the light of history in the writings of Romans and Greeks at around the time when Christ was born. Caesar, Pliny, Tacitus, Strabo and Plutarch all mention it as a country settled by Germanic tribes. These tribes first entered Silesia no less than seven hundred years before the birth of Christ. In the fourth century B.C. came the Celts, and then the Germani again. The Germanic tribes settled there for over a thousand years and developed a civilization and culture whose high level is vouched for by numerous archaeological finds. Down to this day a considerable area of your homeland bears the name of one of these Germanic tribes, the Silingae. It is from them that the name Silesia comes.

In about the year A.D. 600 West Slavic tribes gradually began to infiltrate into an area which had in the meantime become depopulated as a result of the Great Migrations, but it was not until three hundred years later that there was any more permanent Slav settlement. The country now became an apple of discord for the rapidly rising and equally rapidly falling empires of the Moravians, Bohemians and Poles.

Around the middle of the twelfth century Poland began to break up into small principalities. The Silesian Piasta ruling family sought and found support from German Kaisers such as Konrad II and Frederick Barbarossa; and since for generation after generation this family married German wives they became German themselves, even though in many cases they still bore Slav names. But by the thirteenth century they had German names; for example, Heinrich I who ruled in Breslau and Cracow, and was premier Duke of Poland. His mother was a Palatinate Countess from Sulzbach, and his wife was the Countess Hedwig von Andechs-Meran. This was Saint Hedwig, the patroness of Silesia, and down to this day thousands of Silesians make pilgrimages to her birthplace in Bavaria. Her son Duke Heinrich II was killed at the battle of Liegnitz in 1241. Duke Heinrich IV of Breslau was a German minnesinger.

German peasants, craftsmen and monks came into the country and finally they established German law and Western civilization there. In the light of these historical facts we can see that the much-talked-of German 'Drang nach Osten' was a splendid achievement of peaceable settlement. It took place at the wish of the rulers of that country, without the use of the sword, without cruelties, without expulsions, and without oppression.

The German and Polish nobles and their followers fought side by side at Liegnitz against the successors of Genghis Khan, and although most of the defenders were left dead on the field of battle, their sacrifice saved the whole of Europe from the incursions of the Mongols.

It was at this time that the Silesian principalities began to separate from Poland, and up to the middle of the fourteenth century Upper Silesia was independent. In the Treaty of Trentschin in 1335 the Polish King Casimir surrendered his rights in the Silesian Principalities in favour of King John of Bohemia. Twenty years later, after his coronation as Holy Roman Emperor, Karl IV, the son of John, renewed this assimilation. The German Electors now declared Silesia to be an appanage of the Bohemian Crown, and therefore an inseparable part of the German Reich.

Silesia remained attached to the Bohemian Crown for almost four hundred years – first under the Luxemburgers, from 1526 on under the House of Hapsburg, up to 1742 when Silesia was conquered by Frederick the Great. From then on it was part of Germany as a Prussian province.

In these hundred of years, Silesia, together with the Hapsburg lands, developed into a great centre of civilization and culture – as witness the magnificent baroque buildings, monasteries, churches, civic and private edifices, which still stand there in our own day.

When the Polish western frontier as laid down in the Versailles Treaty separated Upper Silesia from the rest of Germany even the Allies of that day thought the claim was of very doubtful validity, and so a plebiscite was arranged. Although it was carried out under pressure from the Korfanty insurrection, tolerated by a far from unsympathetic occupation force, and although the indisputably German areas were not allowed to take part, this plebiscite gave a majority of sixty per cent to Germany, a defeated country. It was this very unambiguous situation which impelled the then British Premier, Lloyd George, to tell the Allied Supreme Council on August 19th 1921 that Upper Silesia, including the plebiscitary area, was only one part of Silesia as a whole, to which it had belonged from time immemorial, with which it formed a historical, economic and cultural whole, and from which it could not be arbitrarily separated. He also pointed out that Upper Silesia had been in German possession for seven hundred years – longer than Normandy had been part of France.

Nevertheless, the Conference of Ambassadors in Geneva in October 1921 decided to dismember Upper Silesia, and a third of the country was granted to the new Polish State. All the deposits of zinc, eighty-five per cent of the coal, and seventy-five per cent of the industrial plant were in the separated third, as also were the towns of Kattowitz and Königshütte, whose inhabitants had voted 85·4 and 74·7 per cent respectively for Germany. The Polish vote at the Reichstag elections in the 'twenties sank to 1·8 per cent in that part of Upper Silesia which had remained German.

Whoever has studied the documents relating to the present Oder-Neisse frontier cannot but conclude that its authors made no attempt to draw it in accordance with historical or ethnographical conditions. Indeed, they have admitted quite openly that such matters were not in their minds.

The German-Polish frontier in Silesia has existed since the Treaty of Trentschin in 1335, and the German-Polish frontier of East Prussia has existed since the Peace of Melnosee in 1422; that is to say, quite a while before the discovery of America. In other words, the eastern frontier of that part of Germany which is now under Polish rule was one of the oldest and most firmly established frontiers in the whole history of Europe.

When Molotov spoke of 'the re-establishment of ancient frontiers in East Prussia and on the Oder' at Yalta, President Roosevelt asked how long it had been since those lands were under Polish rule. Molotov had to admit that it was a very long time indeed, whereupon Roosevelt observed that such reasoning might persuade the English to demand the return of the United States.

The ten million inhabitants of this quarter of German territory were almost one hundred per cent German before 1945; and neither the mass flight before the advancing Red armies, nor the subsequent mass expulsions – the biggest in history – makes any difference to the right of the East Germans to their homeland.

The Oder-Neisse line has nothing whatever to do with historical facts or with the right of self-determination. On the contrary, it is a flagrant violation of Article 2 of the Atlantic Charter, which declares that no frontier changes may take place without the freely-expressed permission of the populations concerned.

The Oder-Neisse Line came about because the Soviet Union wanted to annex those Polish territories to the east of the Curzon Line, and the Poles demanded territorial compensation to the West for the great loss of territory this involved – a unique arrangement in these days of self-determination and anti-colonialism. During the war, and for tactical considerations, the Big Three agreed to this arrangement at the conferences of Teheran and Yalta, but at the Potsdam Conference in August 1945 it was described as a temporary Polish administration of the German Eastern lands. Part B of Article VIII of the minutes of the Potsdam Conference declares:

'The Heads of the three Governments confirm their view that the final settlement of the western frontier of Poland should be left until the peace conference, and they agree that until then the German areas east of the Oder-Neisse line, including the Free Town of Danzig, shall be placed under Polish administration.'

These provisions of the so-called 'Potsdam Agreement' are of fundamental importance for any verdict on the legal situation of the

German eastern areas. They lay down very clearly that the German provinces to the east of the Oder-Neisse line are *de jure* still part of Germany until the final verdict on their fate at a peace conference, even though for the time being and until the final settlement by a treaty of peace, for which we are still waiting, they are to remain under Polish administration.

Even before the Potsdam Conference there was a binding declaration that these areas belong to Germany; namely, in the 'Establishment of Zones of Occupation in Germany' dated June 5th 1945, which divided Germany 'within her own frontiers as they existed on December 31st 1937' for the purposes of occupation by the forces of the four Powers.

President Truman reported to the American people on the Potsdam Conference in a speech delivered on August 9th 1945, and declared that the conference had to some extent been bound in the Polish question by certain agreements made at Yalta; and he went on to say that the Polish Provisional Government had agreed that the final settlement should be left to a peace treaty.

In defiance of this clear and legally acknowledged situation, the communist régime in the Soviet Zone, which has no mandate in free elections and therefore has no right to speak in the name of the German people, signed a so-called treaty on June 6th 1950 with the communist Government of Poland, which, incidentally, has no greater legitimacy, recognizing the Oder-Neisse Line as the ultimate frontier.

The three Western High Commissioners thereupon handed the Soviet Commander-in-Chief in Germany and head of the Foreign Mission, General Zhuikov, a note from the Federal Government protesting against this recognition in the Görlitz Agreement of the Oder-Neisse Line as the definitive eastern frontier of Germany. The note insisted that the areas east of the Oder-Neisse Line were still part and parcel of Germany; that in accordance with the Potsdam Agreement they had been only temporarily handed over to Polish administration as part of the Soviet Zone of occupation; and that Germany's definitive frontiers could be settled only by a peace treaty.

In handing over this note the Allied High Commission also stressed that according to the Potsdam Agreement the frontiers of Germany were to be definitively fixed by a treaty of peace, and that therefore it must regard the agreement between the Soviet Zone

Republic and the Polish Government in Görlitz as a breach of the Four Power Agreement.

The Federal Government also published a protest on June 9th 1950 in which it said:

'The so-called Government of the Soviet Zone has no right whatsoever to speak in the name of the German people. All its agreements are therefore null and void. The final decision regarding Germany's eastern territories at present under Polish and Soviet administration will be taken in a peace treaty signed with Germany as a whole. Acting on behalf of the whole German people the Federal Government will never recognize the annexation of purely German territories, and protests that it violates all canons of justice and humanity. At future peace negotiations the Federal Government will plead for a just solution between a really democratic Poland and a democratic and united Germany.'

Speaking at a special session of the first German Federal Parliament, its Social-Democrat President, Paul Löbe, himself a Silesian, made a similar declaration in the name of all the Federal Länder Governments and of the Federal Council, of all parliamentary Parties, except the Communists, and of the Germans living in the Soviet zone of occupation:

'In accordance with the Potsdam Agreement, the German territory east of the Oder-Neisse Line has been temporarily placed under Polish administration as a part of the Soviet zone of occupation. The territory remains part of Germany. No one has the right to make arbitrary arrangements to dispose of territory and people.'

On June 7th 1950 a representative of the Foreign Office in London declared that the Oder-Neisse Line had never been accepted as the definitive frontier. The three Western Powers had never recognized the ceding of any German territory to Poland. The British attitude had not changed since Potsdam, and Stalin himself had declared on July 21st 1945 that the final decision regarding the Polish Western frontier could be reached only when a German Peace Treaty was signed. The British Foreign Secretary, Ernest Bevin, had expressed his approval of this attitude at the Conference of Foreign Ministers in Moscow in 1947. The British Government would therefore ignore the Görlitz Agreement and regard it as non-existent.

On June 8th 1950 a representative of the American State Department described the arrangement come to two days previously between the administration of the Soviet Zone and communist Poland as a violation of the Potsdam Agreement, declaring that the matters at issue could not be settled by representatives of the existing régime in East Germany since they had no real democratic basis and could under no circumstances speak in the name of the German people. At no time had the United States Government ever recognized the Oder-Neisse Line as the definitive eastern frontier of Germany, and it did not recognize the present arrangement between the Polish Government and the East German administration.

And on July 7th 1950 the Quai d'Orsay issued the following statement:

'The French Foreign Ministry empowers its High Commissioner in Germany to declare that France expressly recognizes the German frontiers of 1937, and that she recognizes the German Federal Government, formed as the result of free elections, as the representative of all Germany.'

Similar declarations from neutral sources would fill volumes, and one and all they confirm the *de jure* status of Germany's eastern territories. They prove that Germany's claim in this matter is not an aggressive, nationalistic demand, but that it derives from a desire for a just solution which alone can guarantee a lasting peace.

Denouncing the dead dictator at the Twentieth Congress of the Communist Party of the Soviet Union on February 25th 1956, Khrushchev justly blamed Stalin for the monstrous mass deportations carried out in the Soviet Union, and condemned them as 'a brutal violation of the principles of equality and friendship between the nationalities of the Soviet Union.' He went on to say that it was beyond understanding that whole peoples, including women and children and old people, should be made responsible for the acts of individuals, and vengefully subjected to such mass misery and suffering.

But in his indictment of his former master, Khrushchev did not mention Stalin's proposal at Yalta for mass deportations from Germany's eastern territories, though they were unprecedented in number. When they were ultimately carried out it was not by Stalin

99

alone, of course. But, to borrow Khrushchev's words, those deportations were also 'a brutal violation of the principles of equality and friendship between nations'.

On April 8th the *Observer* published a letter from the Bishop of Chichester commenting on the visit of the Soviet Security chief Serov to Britain and recalling the mass deportation of East Germans from their homes and their homeland. He also recalled that a deputation of high prelates had waited on Prime Minister Attlee in September 1945 to express their horror at the actions of the Polish and Russian Governments; and that the Synods of Canterbury and York in October 1945 had adopted protest resolutions, condemning the eviction of German families from their homes and their homelands in East Germany and the Sudeten area as a deplorable violation of those principles of humanity the Allies had undertaken to uphold.

These British prelates asked the British Government to continue to urge the Governments of Soviet Russia, Poland and Czechoslovakia to bring these scandals to an end. The Bishop of Chichester also recalled his own protest in the House of Lords on January 30th 1946 against the cruelty of the deportations carried out in pursuance of the Yalta and Potsdam agreements. His letter concluded:

> 'There could be few greater services to the cause of unity and peace than a repudiation by his successors of the policy adopted under Stalin's leadership at Yalta . . . and the results which have followed.'

Speaking on April 21st 1956 to newspaper publishers, President Eisenhower declared that there would have to be fundamental changes in Soviet policy before it would be possible for the free peoples to relax their vigilance. Although some things had changed in the Soviet Union, injustices committed by Stalin against other peoples were being perpetuated by his successors.

Despite all the efforts of the West in Berlin and Geneva Germany was still divided thanks to the Soviet veto against free German elections. The satellite peoples of Eastern Europe were still pawns in the Soviet game. Our efforts to remedy such injustices and to resolve the questions that still divided the world must not be allowed to slacken. President Eisenhower then went on to say that the United States was prepared to explore every avenue in the hope of arriving at a peaceable remedy for such slavery and the unjust dismemberment of nations that had once been free.

A few days later on May 1st 1956 I spoke in much the same way at a meeting of the Foreign Press Association in London. If more attention had been paid to my remarks there, in answer to questions put by the journalists present, it would have been less easy to misrepresent my attitude to these problems now. I pointed out that 'the dangerous tension which exists between the two world groups has been caused by the unfortunate heritage of unsolved problems and unconscionable injustices left behind by the war.'

We have heard a good deal lately of the terrible mistakes Stalin made in his own country, as I pointed out whilst I was in London, and now we are waiting to see a few of his foreign-political mistakes corrected too.

What I said on May 1st I now repeat on July 1st. And we are not the only ones who are waiting. To the voice of the American President and that of the Bishop of Chichester let me add that of a prominent Prince of the Catholic Church. In January 1956, Francis Spellman, Cardinal-Archbishop of New York, sent a message of greetings to the Easter Conference of Sudeten Germans in Nuremberg in which he declared that the great strength of the free world lay in its unity. He felt, he declared, that those who had been forced to leave their countries, including those who had been driven out on account of their beliefs, should unite their efforts with those of the Sudeten Germans to attain their common objective. The support given by the Sudeten Germans to the idea of a Central European community was a step in the right direction. The land they were now living in had given them protection and shelter for the time being, and this gesture deserved deep gratitude. However, their return to their own homeland remained not only the right, but the duty of all those people who had been driven away from their homes, and all their efforts should be directed to this ultimate aim. In the meantime Divine Justice should be a source of strength and hope for all displaced Germans.

Cardinal Spellman was writing in the same spirit as that of the Papal memorandum of March 1st 1948. The Holy Father declared the driving of the East Germans out of their homes and their lands as 'a happening unexampled in history', and he continued:

'We think we know what happened between the Vistula and the Volga during the war years, but was it right to take revenge by driving twelve million people from their homes and plunging them

101

into distress and misery? And was that measure politically reasonable and economically responsible if we bear in mind the vital necessities of the German people, and, over and above this, the interests of Europe as a whole? We sincerely hope that all those concerned will come to a calmer view and repair the damage as far as it can still be repaired.'

There is nothing I need add to this plea from an authoritative centre of our culture and civilization.

We cannot recall to life the million dead who were victims of these tremendous mass expulsions any more than we can the victims with which the National Socialist régime stained the good name of our country.

The reconstruction of the East Germany that is separated from us today will be like rebuilding the ruined towns – a task that we have begun but by no means finished yet. Even if the land remains, the landscape will take on a different face.

The preliminary condition for this reconstruction is a peaceable solution, and only a peace treaty can bring that. The contracting party on our side can only be an all-German Government deriving its authority from free elections. For this, amongst other important reasons, the union of Central and West Germany is the most urgent problem of reunification that now occupies us, since no one can walk through a closed door.

Believe me, we are carefully examining these difficult matters in a full realization of the tremendous responsibility we have to carry. Let me therefore repeat in conclusion what I said a few days ago in the name of the Federal Government in the Federal parliament:

'The Federal Government has never resigned itself to the partition of Germany, and it maintains its very clear attitude to the question of our eastern frontiers.'

I attach particular importance to this observation because a remark I made at a press conference in London has been wrongly interpreted. The Federal Government has never reconciled itself to the partition of Germany, and in full accord with the declared will of the German people it has repeatedly insisted that the frontiers of 1937 are still valid, and that no unilateral decisions taken in the years of collapse are recognized by the German people. The right to their homeland and the right to self-determination are inalienable conditions for any settlement of the problem of those who have been exiled, or who are now living without freedom.

The Federal Government has therefore solemnly repeated that the solution of the problem of Germany's eastern frontiers must be left to a treaty of peace, and that can be signed only by an all-German Government democratically authorized by the whole German people. This attitude does not clash with the repeatedly confirmed assurance that neither the Federal Government nor the German people will ever seek to secure their rights by force. I said this once again on May 1st in London. The Federal Government regards the creation of a permanent peace on the basis of law and justice as between Germany and her neighbours as a truly European task. The charter of those driven from their homes, which was adopted on August 5th 1950 in Stuttgart, breathes this same spirit of neighbourly reconciliation. The accredited representatives of millions of expelled Germans did not content themselves with affirming their right to self-determination, but they also announced their 'solemn and sacred decision, having regard to the infinite suffering the past decade has brought to humanity, to renounce all thought of vengeance'.

The Federal Government feels that it is in no way compromising the free decision of any future all-German Government when, in the name of the whole German people, it expresses its sincere desire to arrive at a peaceable understanding with its Eastern-European neighbours too. At the same time it underlines the main principle of its whole foreign policy: namely, to seek a settlement of all disputes by peaceable agreement between free peoples, living together not with feelings of hatred and mistrust, or desire for vengeance, but with a sincere desire for peace and their joint welfare.

A word about our Polish neighbours: despite the events of recent years, it is a fact that there have rarely been two neighbouring States which have so seldom come to blows. For almost a thousand years Germans and Poles worked together in the interests of their common Christian and European civilization, and they were joined together by innumerable historical, economic, cultural and even family bonds. Hardly anywhere is this so clear as it is in your homeland Upper Silesia.

It was only when an extreme form of nationalism began to dominate European thought that conflict and hatred separated the two peoples. The amoral dismemberment of Poland carried out in the eighteenth century was not the will of the German people, and in the nineteenth century they rejoiced at the Polish movement for liberty.

The more the two neighbouring peoples remember what they have in common, and the more European their thoughts, the less inclined they will be to fight each other and the more clearly they will recognize that the spirit of nationalism must be overcome in Eastern Europe to make way for the spirit of the European community. Incidentally, we are very well aware that it is the will of the Polish people to belong to Europe, and for our part we should not like to see a free Europe without them.

By acting in a European spirit the Federal Government is now doing its best to resolve the bitter conflicts which have separated us from our Western neighbours for so long, but before we can take the same fruitful path in Eastern Europe two conditions must be fulfilled. The first is that all concerned should show good will and the desire to find solutions not based on injustice. In my opinion, the expulsion of millions of people and the annexation of territory historically belonging to another country cannot be the basis for a permanent settlement since they violate all the tenets of natural, human and divine law. However, a just solution – and this is the second condition – can be agreed to only between free peoples. Today the Polish people are not free. A totalitarian Government, illegitimate at home and dependent abroad – one which has quite recently used machine-guns and tanks against its own working people, as in Posen – will never be in a position even to strive for a just solution. One of the main planks in Stalin's foreign policy was to chain Poland to Russia by offering her a quarter of Germany's territory.

We are unfortunately not in a position to fulfil the two preliminary conditions I have mentioned, although, of course, our attitude can encourage or hamper a constructive settlement.

In the past few years those who have been expelled from their homes have given us all an example of discipline and achievement, and in doing so they have helped to save our people from communist slavery; by their patience they have rendered great service to the cause of Europe and the free world. Thanks to the spirit of reconciliation which, despite all their sufferings, is expressed in the charter of those who have been driven from their homes, they have shown the way to all men of good will. We must continue along this path and do our best to bring about a world in which all peoples will be able to live in peace and freedom – and on friendly terms with their neighbours.

104

# 11

## The Right of Germans to Self-Determination*

I AM particularly glad to be able to address you today because I know what a heavy burden you have had to carry during the past ten years as people who have been driven from your homeland. You have shared this fate with millions of Germans from our eastern territories, and with millions of other people all over the world. The problem created by these mass expulsions has now become one which is of interest to the whole world and calls out for a permanent ethical, ethnographical and political solution. The basis of any just solution must be the right of the individual to self-determination in his own homeland, and the firm intention to make this a permanent part of international law for the future.

What exactly do we mean by homeland? The old idea that it means just the neighbourhood we were brought up in is no longer adequate. The familiar mother tongue, customs, laws and religious beliefs – indeed, the whole complex of human relationships in our daily lives, all belong to our idea of homeland. Your lives have been torn out of this whole environment, and in the meantime conditions in your homeland have been greatly changed because it has been forced into the totalitarian system of the Soviet Bloc. One day, the Iron Curtain will finally rise, but it will not be possible to restore things in Eastern and Central Europe just as they were when you were driven out of your homeland. When the day of reunion finally comes, both those who went and those who stayed behind will have – as, indeed, we all shall – to adapt themselves to new conditions and join together to create a new homeland. There is no doubt

*Speech delivered on July 22nd 1956 in Königstein to the Ackermann Society, an association of Sudeten German Catholics.

105

that we shall have to abandon certain deeply-rooted ideas, as, indeed, we have already had to do; but to build up the future means to look with new eyes and not allow ourselves to be blinded by the past.

To make it easier to understand what I mean let me briefly recall the history of that part of Central Europe in which your homeland is situated. From the first period in which Eastern Central Europe became conscious of itself as an entity, its political and cultural development was always determined by whatever spiritual and political powers happened at the time to be dominant: the Church in Rome on one hand, and Byzantium, later Moscow, on the other; the Carolingian, later the Holy Roman Empire, and its spiritual heritage, the rising Russian empire in the East with its centre in Moscow. There were frequent attempts to create political centres and large territorial conglomerations in Central Europe. Bohemia and Poland both tried, and there were also Prussian and Austro-Hungarian attempts at a solution. But the one really fundamental decision had already been arrived at early on in the Middle Ages: culturally Central Europe belongs to the European West. This is a historical tradition we should never neglect. Charles the Great incorporated Bohemia, Moravia and the territories between the Elbe and the Oder up to the Middle Danube in his empire. This was the first drive of the West, which was then repeated later under the Ottos and the Hohenstaufen, and added the territory up to the Drave to the Holy Roman Empire. On this political basis the Catholic Church then converted the peoples of these territories and attached them firmly to the Western Christian world while the Byzantine Church brought the countries and peoples of the Balkans and of Russia under its sway.

It was of great importance for the cultural attachment of these Central European areas to the Western world that from the late Middle Ages German settlers streamed into them. They did not go sword in hand to conquer foreign territory, but at the invitation of the reigning princes of those lands to clear the frontier forests and found German towns and villages.

The historical significance of this East-German settlement lies primarily in this unique achievement. In those days the fact that German territory extended eastward, and that these countries, including your own homeland, thus harboured two different peoples, was no problem, because the conception of the Christian Middle Ages was universal; but it was to lead to political complications later.

Despite internal tension and conflicts this world was politically and culturally well integrated, but as Europe left the Middle Ages to enter the modern age, a new factor arose – the national awakening of individual peoples. It would be quite wrong to look at this development one-sidedly from the angle of Central and Eastern Europe only, and to condemn everything that took place as a result of this development as false and undesirable. On the contrary, a spiritual movement of great importance began with the Renaissance in Italy, and was subsequently continued in Spain, France and England; and still later, in the eighteenth century, in Germany. In the nineteenth and twentieth centuries it began to rouse up the peoples of Central and Eastern Europe too. In our own day this movement is being continued outside Europe. It brings people to a recognition of their own specific qualities, and it leads to the rise of nationalism, with all its opportunities and dangers. It has produced a great number of national and individual achievements which none of us would like to see removed from the history of Europe and the world. In Eastern Europe, this development to nationhood, and to the language consciousness of even the smallest people, goes back to a German, Herder, though it would certainly be unfair to regard him as the father of any narrow-minded nationalism. He certainly cannot be blamed for the symptoms of degeneration which subsequently made themselves felt. What he had in view was a fruitful symbiosis of Germany's intellectual life with that of her European neighbours, and I feel that we have every cause to be proud of him and his work.

However, we cannot welcome the political consequences of this development with the same approval. In Western and Central Europe the greater unity of the Middle Ages was broken up and gave way to a welter of national States sealed off from each other. A sort of political balance developed amongst them, but from time to time it was disturbed by the efforts of one nation or the other to establish its hegemony – first there was Spain, then Holland and France, and finally Germany. The culmination of this reckless and degenerate nationalism – there was little true national spirit left – took place under Hitler. It has turned the whole of Europe into a field of tension with the United States on the one side and the Soviet Union on the other as opposing centres of attraction. One of its results is that the line which divides Europe now goes right through our Fatherland. If Europe wishes to continue to exist as a representative of Western Christian civilization then it cannot be based on the old jumble of national States in which the strongest will from time to time seek to establish its hegemony.

In that area from which you come it proved particularly impossible, owing to the overlapping settlements, to found really homogeneous national States, though unfortunately this did not mean that no attempt was made to found them, but merely that the conflicts between peoples continued to exist within these new States, even when they were relatively small. The relationship of the particular majority people to the German minority group, which was often quite large, was often very difficult. However, we should not forget that similar difficulties were present in other border areas.

The kind of situation that developed from about the beginning of the nineteenth century on will be known to the older ones amongst you from your own experience. The insistence of the particular majority groups that their political influence should be dominant, and that their particular national civilization should be privileged at the expense of other and no less valuable though different minority civilizations naturally aroused resistance on the part of these other national groups, particularly when they happened to have held the lead politically and spiritually in the former older and larger States. The general result was, as we know only too well, resentment, excessive national touchiness, arrogance, and an exaggerated – one might say even perverted – nationalism. All of this gave rise to endless trouble, and finally led to the tragic and violent solutions of our own day; to the attempt to settle matters once and for all, and establish clearly-defined national relationships by driving out the German minorities and ignoring the rights of individuals and of whole national groups to their homes and to their way of life. You and the others who have lost their homes and their homeland in Eastern and Central Europe are not the only sufferers. If such behaviour becomes normal – and it has already been copied in other parts of the world – the whole of mankind will suffer, because it is a violation of the fundamental rights of man. The moral and political confusion to which this sort of thing will lead unless humanity sets its face against it with determination is unimaginable.

The happenings of 1945 and 1946 show very clearly, however, that when you return, as we all hope you will, it will not be possible to resume things as they were before 1945. We have not, in fact, been able to do that in any sphere of German political life. We can find no solution for the future on the basis of past ideas: the nationalist ideologies of the nineteenth century with their national struggles. We must find solutions which will guarantee freedom, human dignity and their own way of life to all national, religious and other groups, and the individuals in them, while at the same time taking the exigencies of large-scale political and economic developments into account.

I am aware that this necessity has already been recognized and accepted by you, as shown by the charter you adopted when you formed your organization.* I also know that as a whole both the Sudeten Germans and the East Germans who have been driven from their homes accept its principles, and solemnly renounce all thought of vengeance.

This applies to the Federal Government and to the whole German people too. Speaking in the Federal Diet a few weeks ago, and a little later in Bochum before 80,000 Germans from Upper Silesia,† I took occasion to announce solemnly that neither the Federal Government nor the German people – of which you are part – will ever use violence to attain even their just claims. But it is equally true to say that the expulsion of millions of people and the violation of right and justice can never be recognized as a basis on which to build the future. Under the auspices of a free and Christian Europe and with good will and determination on both sides a free German people and a free Czech people will find a solution for the Sudeten problem which will allow you to return to your homes and work there for the benefit of both our peoples. Such a Europe will not be a unitarian State of unorganized individuals of different languages, but a close community of national States. However, a national State as the basis for such a community of States will not be the end of the development. The national State is the edifice incorporating the family, the homeland and the community as the basis, and protected by the European community as the general roof. Europe and its individual member States will live together according to the principle of subsidiary function; that is to say, a task will be undertaken by the next highest level only when the lower level cannot carry it out with its own resources. We believe that such a State and such a Europe will make it possible for the first time for free individuals, free families, free national groups and free peoples to live together peaceably.

*The Charter of those Germans who have been driven from their homes was adopted by their organizations in August 1950. It solemnly renounced all thoughts of vengeance and called for the recognition of the right to a homeland as one of the fundamental rights granted to man by God.

†See page 92.

During the public debates which have taken place recently you were told that people who said only what they knew you wanted to hear were not necessarily your best friends, and this is very true. It is neither easy nor agreeable to tell people that their hopes may never be fulfilled, to tell people who are longing to return to their homeland that they should do their best to settle down in their new homes and forget the longing for their old homeland in constructive work. It is not always easy to take a stand against nationalistic slogans, to persuade people to face the realities of political life, and to appeal to them for peace and reconciliation instead of revenge. But those who have the political responsibility – no matter in what place or in what group – must never forget that we have a Fatherland in common and that the interests of all must be reconciled. It doesn't really help you when people tell you what you want to hear, even though it cannot be achieved in reality. But of one thing you may be confident, so long as Federal Chancellor Doctor Adenauer is responsible for the Government, and, allow me to add, so long as I guide the affairs of the Foreign Office, your interests will be our interests. When I left the Federal Chancellor last night after telling him that I should be talking to you today he asked me to bring you his greetings and assure you that we should never forget your interests. Those words were said from the heart. And when other people approach you then ask yourselves who is more likely to stand up for your interests. Our task at the moment is that we should work together to secure and maintain freedom in our own country, because only if we remain free ourselves can we possibly hope to bring freedom to those who have lost it. Only if we are determined to defend our country will it be possible one day for free men to leave their new homeland and return to their old.

# 12

# Problems of Foreign Policy Concerning Co-operation with the Under-developed Countries*

LATEST happenings in the Near East show very clearly that the world is in a widespread process of political, sociological and economic transformation in which the so-called under-developed countries are playing a very special role.

These countries, whose inhabitants represent about half the population of the globe and whose territories represent about half its area, are going through a very profound development. Not so long ago they were largely objects of the political action of the world; now they are beginning to develop actively and play to some extent an independent role. At the same time they are moved by a great urge for emancipation and freedom, and for recognition and prestige.

Having won their political freedom these peoples now want to develop their economy in order to protect it, to raise their standards of living, and to enjoy the benefits of science and technology.

The Soviet Union is seeking to exploit this situation in order to draw these countries into its own orbit. The methods it adopts are many and varied, but its final aim is always the same: World Communism. Its propaganda against 'Capitalist Imperialism' is linked with an economic offensive of its own aimed at extending its influence over these countries.

Whether these under-developed countries will overcome their backwardness successfully, and whether in the process they organize themselves on Western or on Communist lines, will depend on whether the Western World recognizes the magnitude of the task

*Speech delivered on November 24th 1956 to the Society for Economic Progress in Baden-Wurtemberg.

111

which faces it and the gravity of the challenge the bolshevist world is throwing down, and acts accordingly.

The under-developed countries are neither communist nor Western as such. What they want is to be free of hunger, disease and economic distress; they want to raise their living standards and strengthen themselves politically, economically and culturally. Whether they will choose dictatorship or democracy is still undecided.

To influence this decision is one of the most important tasks of the age, and it goes far beyond short-term world-political decisions. It demands constructive thought and an understanding of different forms of civilization and unprecedented situations. It is not even primarily a question of the struggle against Communism, or, indeed, against anything. Our task is to develop constructive forms of a social and economic system which will be in accordance with Western libertarian ideas and which will at the same time satisfy the reasonable expectations of the under-developed countries, and contribute to the essential pacification of the world.

Whilst understanding the desire for 'development', both we and the under-developed countries need a certain dose of scepticism in face of the widespread assumption that development is the equivalent of progress, and that 'development' as such is necessarily positive and creative.

In our co-operation with these peoples we should refrain from trying to develop them exclusively according to our own ideas, and from giving them exclusively advice based on our own experience, since this may not be what they need at all. At the same time it is quite clear that we can and must help, but such help will be really useful only if we and they share the responsibility for individually appropriate solutions. As far as we are concerned this means an acknowledgement that our own social and economic form of development is not the only possible one and, indeed, need not necessarily be ultimately adopted. For the under-developed countries it means the abandonment of the widespread illusion of forced modernization. Illusions on either side can do untold damage.

According to our ideas the best way to deal with surplus population is by rapidly increasing industrialism, but the situation which existed in the Western World during its industrialization is not the same as that which now exists in the under-developed countries. For a long time now the whole population increase in the West has been absorbed by industry and other non-agricultural occupations, but in the under-developed countries the growth of the population is so large that modern industry with its decreasing labour-power requirements can absorb only a fraction of it. Balanced growth in all respects must therefore be aimed at. Unless agricultural production increases new industries cannot flourish, and vice-versa.

It also seems undesirable to pump millions into these countries in order to develop excessive industrialization and mechanization when the only result can be to transform an agricultural population at present living in a hierarchical order into a rootless industrial proletariat. That would be encouraging precisely what we wish to avoid: driving them into the arms of Communism. A rootless industrial proletariat, even if it enjoys high standards of living, is far more likely to provide a basis for political radicalism than a rural population, even if its living standards are low.

The extent to which agriculture can be mechanized in these countries is narrowly limited. It is the intensive manual cultivation of the soil that saves the population from starvation and the soil from impoverishment. In this situation any excessive mechanization would close up the only outlet for labour-power and release it to no purpose.

Thus if we really want to help the under-developed countries we must assist them to an 'organic' development.

We should also not seek to impose our own ideas with regard to the relationship between the State and the economy where the under-developed countries are concerned. It is, of course, tempting for the liberal economist of the West to suppose that a market economy is the only possible form of co-operation with these countries, but this overlooks the fact that in many respects the situation there is very different from that of the industrial countries of the West, and that in consequence the State there will have a bigger role to play in economic life than we should think desirable in the conditions existing in our own countries. For example, there is no lively capital market in the under-developed countries, no long-established middle class, and no already highly-developed branches of industry to be the instruments for further construction. This means that the Government there will have to do many things which we leave as a matter of course to private enterprise in our countries. As it is, the industrial and the under-developed countries must co-operate in the finding of the individually appropriate solutions.

However, if this is to be done successfully then, on their part, the under-developed countries must create confidence in the stability and continuation of development, and confidence, above all, that agreements entered into will also be honoured. As things stand it is significant that voluntary capital exports to these countries are far from satisfactory. The increase during the past few years was by no means commensurate with the growing economic prosperity of the world. On the other hand it would be wrong to argue that because voluntary capital export is unsatisfactory, and the situation urgent, therefore public money should be spent. If confidence is lacking then in the long run the provision of public money won't help either. The under-developed countries must take steps to encourage private capitalist investment in their territories, refrain from sequestration, and create security against special risks by allowing monetary transfer, and so on.

Economic aid can be given to the under-developed countries in the form of long-term investment, long-term credits, long-term purchasing arrangements, and technological help.

Both 'political' and 'economic' aid can be granted. Economic aid granted for political reasons has strings attached. 'General economic aid' aims at strengthening the economic potential of the under-developed countries. Such aid may be regarded as a permanent constructive factor in our present-day world economic order.

'Political economic aid' is a supplementary conception made necessary by the political tension existing in the world at the present time.

As a general rule the under-developed countries welcome only this purely economic aid, because they feel that in the last resort it serves the interests of both parties, and creates a permanent basis of mutual interest on which further economic development can take place.

It is desirable therefore that this 'general economic aid' should be the rule, and 'political economic aid' the exception determined by a given political situation.

The major part of Western economic co-operation with the under-developed countries is carried out by private capitalist enterprise, and private arrangements are come to without any political strings.

The situation where the Soviet Bloc is concerned is very different. In the last resort every arrangement these countries make with the under-developed countries is political, and behind it is Bolshevism, which attaches great importance to increasing its influence on the under-developed countries and regards economic aid as one of the best ways of achieving this. The real aim of the so-called economic offensive of the Soviet Bloc is to facilitate communist efforts in the under-developed countries.

However, communization is not the immediate aim in these countries, and no doubt the communist planners are realistic enough to foresee that opposition to anything of that sort would be too strong. The immediate aim is to turn countries which tend to be pro-Western, or at least truly neutral, into 'neutralist' countries, in the hope that once the West has been squeezed out it will be merely a question of time before these countries can be turned into satellites.

The Soviet system has unquestionably certain preliminary advantages in its drive to break into the under-developed countries. Where they have gained their independence these countries want to reinforce it by economic independence, so the communists assure them that when the West offers aid it is merely striving to replace the old political dependence of the colonialist system by economic dependence on capitalism, whereas, they claim, the Soviet Union is 'fraternally prepared to share its last crust' with them.

Further, the Soviet Union claims to afford a model of 'how to do it' to the under-developed countries, since only a generation back Russia herself was an under-developed country, and has since, in a relatively short period, achieved just what the under-developed countries now so ardently desire.

At the same time the Soviet Union seeks to make a virtue of its own agricultural difficulties. The agricultural production of the Soviet Bloc has not kept up with the forced industrialization, and so the Soviet Union is very willing to come forward as a permanent buyer of agricultural produce from the under-developed countries. In this respect the West is at a disadvantage, since its agricultural surpluses are so great that its chief problem is to know what to do with them.

And another point is that the question of production costs plays a role in Western economic arrangements with the under-developed countries, and places a limit on concessions. This is not so with the Soviet Union, which is quite prepared at all times not only to subordinate economic to political considerations, but to ignore economic considerations altogether if necessary.

Where the West is concerned the rivalry of national industries and firms, or question of national prestige, can hinder the rational

115

exploitation of any given situation, whereas the Soviet Union can centrally impose a division of labour amongst its satellites.

Recognizing these possibilities and the advantage of mixing commerce and politics which is natural to a government-controlled economic system, the Soviet Bloc opened up an economic offensive in the under-developed countries a few years back. Generally speaking the first stage of the infiltration was in the form of a barter agreement, relating perhaps to one commodity only. If things went well this would be followed by a bilateral agreement, usually associated with a payments agreement. Generally speaking these preliminary arrangements were not fully implemented, because their aim in the first place was propagandist rather than practical, and so big figures and lavish promises were the rule. During the past two years, however, there has been a definite tendency to make such agreements more practical, and to ensure that real commodity movements take place in consequence. At the same time there is also a tendency to extend the term of the agreements with a view to binding the partner more securely.

For some time now there have also been purchases of surplus raw materials and foodstuffs under these agreements. Whenever the under-developed countries have difficulty in disposing of such surpluses, crises develop, and then the countries of the Soviet Bloc come forward as saviours and offer to take the surpluses. They can do this fairly readily because the nature of the Soviet economic system makes it easier to distribute such surpluses. In this way the countries of the Soviet Bloc buy cotton from Egypt, rubber from Ceylon, fruit from the Lebanon, sugar from Cuba, and rice from Burma. Usually an attempt is made to fix up agreements for several years in succession, thus bolstering up the economy of the country in question. In such cases it is easy for the Soviet Bloc countries to present themselves as 'friends in need' to countries allegedly hardpressed by 'capitalist exploitation'.

This Soviet economic offensive extends to all the under-developed countries, including the Near East, Asia, Africa and Latin America. Special efforts are being made to establish positions in the Near and Middle East, and there are obvious reasons for this. For one thing, the area is close at hand, and for another, the Soviets are familiar with Asiatic ways. The Suez trouble is, of course, being widely exploited, and the general assumption is that Soviet arms deliveries will be followed up by long-term trading agreements.

116

The main weight of the Soviet economic offensive is directed towards Egypt, the Sudan, Syria and the Lebanon, and secondarily to India, Burma and Indonesia, with Afghanistan, which is, of course, particularly subject to Soviet influence.

Soviet economic aid embraces both capital and 'technological' assistance, and favourable repayment conditions are the rule. In what the Soviets regard as important agreements, interest and amortization conditions are so favourable that the political character of the arrangement becomes transparent. Interest ranging between two and two and a half per cent, with amortization payments ranging over ten years and even more, and even then beginning only when the plant, or whatever it is, is completed, are terms with which no Western group or firm could possibly compete.

However, it is particularly interesting to note that the Soviet Bloc countries are not prepared to allow the under-developed countries finance *à fonds perdus*. Their slogan is 'trade not aid', and they would like to persuade their partners that although the credit conditions they offer are extraordinarily favourable there is really no question of political strings.

One of the trump cards of the Soviet Bloc countries in their efforts to win over the under-developed countries is the offer of 'technical aid': the provision of technical, managerial or scientific know-how, and practical experience in the use of modern techniques. One has only to remember how closely the superiority of the West is linked up with its technical skills in the eyes of the under-developed peoples, and how anxious they are to master such skills themselves, to realize the importance of this question of 'technological aid'. In the long run business will go to those who do more than just sell machinery, and are prepared to follow up sales with technical assistance. Obviously, anyone who has been trained at a Soviet technical college will prefer Soviet machinery to any other. The Soviet Union sends out its technicians as missionaries, and it also grants stipends to allow young people from the under-developed countries to study at Soviet technical schools. In fact there is no doubt that technological assistance is regarded as the main plank in the Soviet economic offensive, and that the Communists are determined to become the mentors of youth in the under-developed countries both in technology and politics to a far greater extent than the West.

The West, of course, is not indifferent to the needs of the under-developed countries. On the contrary, it was helping long before the

Soviet economic offensive began. This Western assistance takes on many different forms: bilateral, multilateral, and through international organizations.

The Americans with their Four-Point and Foreign-Aid Programmes were the first to give the under-developed countries economic and technological assistance.

The 'Extended Technical Aid Programme' of the United Nations is perhaps the best known of the international efforts. Over seventy countries, including our own, are co-operating in this programme, which places the technical skills and experience, and the training facilities of the industrial countries at the disposal of the under-developed countries. The countries of the Soviet Bloc take only a very limited share in this programme, and their contributions do not amount to more than $4\frac{1}{2}$ per cent of the total cost.

The Colombo Plan, which originated with the Commonwealth, aims at providing capital and technical assistance to a particular area: namely, East and South-East Asia. Capital aid is generally given in the form of grants or loans, and Britain helps by releasing the sterling balances which accumulated during the war to the credit of India, Pakistan and Ceylon. Technical aid is also given by supplying and training technicians.

The European Economic Council is responsible for joint aid to the under-developed partner countries in the Mediterranean area, and the Productivity Centre of the Organization for European Economic Co-operation has been instructed to study the problem of granting technical aid. The World Bank in particular, and also the recently founded International Finance Corporation, provides the under-developed countries with capital on a commercial basis. The chief role of the World Bank is to provide loans to finance key projects for power stations, transport and communications.

Where its statutes prevent the World Bank from assisting, the International Finance Corporation steps in. This is a typical example of the systematic efforts being made in the West to persuade private capital and private firms to invest in the under-developed countries.

The General Agreement on Tariffs and Trade (GATT) also encourages the economic development of these countries by allowing them to deviate from the general conditions of the agreement, and by granting them certain tariff and import privileges.

Finally, the European Economic Commission is studying other

possibilities of assistance in a number of under-developed countries.

In view of the economic importance of this co-operation with the under-developed countries, and also, of course, because of the intensified efforts of the Soviet Bloc countries to gain economic and political influence in these countries, these various organizations in the West have for the past year or so been very closely studying the whole question of aid. Both NATO from a political angle, and the OEEC from a purely economic angle, have been examining the possibilities of increasing this joint aid, and, in particular, what can be done to counter the politico-economic activities of the Soviet Bloc countries.

It must be admitted that the economic offensive of the Soviet Bloc has met with some success in a number of the under-developed countries, though so far – economically considered – it does not represent any very serious problem, since to date the trading turn-over of the Soviet Bloc with these countries is very small.

Without wishing to underestimate the danger that might develop from this Soviet economic offensive, it is a fact that every under-price delivery, and every present made by the Soviet Union for political reasons, has to be paid for: they slow down the rate of increase of Soviet living standards, of Soviet investments, and of the Soviet production apparatus.

Further, every Soviet delivery that increases productive capacity or raises living standards, strengthens the under-developed country in question as a potential supplier to and buyer from the West. Quite generally, Soviet aid releases potential for other purposes, including purchases from the West.

Finally, the general mistrust of 'politico-economic aid' which is prevalent in the under-developed countries also applies to such aid when it comes from the Soviet Bloc countries.

However, there is no doubt that the efforts made so far by the Soviet Union are only a beginning; and the countries of the Soviet Bloc will certainly exploit recent happenings in the Near East for their own purposes.

We should not, of course, allow our co-operation with the under-developed countries to be determined solely by Soviet actions. That is to say, we should not merely stage 'counter-actions'. What we undertake should be based on our own ideas and principles in order to help the under-developed countries to find a solution of their own to their problems.

In particular we should not answer the Soviet economic offensive with one of our own, because the Soviet countries enjoy the advantages of 'the inner line', and they would be in a position to dictate the rules of the game and keep us scurrying around at will. The less the Soviet Bloc engages in real deliveries the easier it will be to impress the under-developed countries with sham offers, or to act as welcome 'price cutters'. As a matter of fact it is in our interests that the Soviet Bloc should be taken at its word in the matter of deliveries. Our technical products need not fear comparison, and there is a great danger for the Soviets that they will bite off more than they can chew.

In any case, we cannot, and do not want to, use the methods of the Soviet Bloc. Even if the Soviet Union should gain preliminary successes thanks to its controlled economy, this should not tempt us to abandon our market-economy principles. In the long run co-operation on a private-capitalist basis is the best way to persuade the under-developed countries that we have no ulterior political motives.

Measures to assist these countries and counter Soviet activities can be really effective only if the West conducts them jointly. If each Western country acts on its own then overlapping is inevitable. In addition, measures carried out on a national basis and independent of other measures are more likely to lead to mistrust and rivalry. Co-operation between the countries of the West is therefore urgently necessary not only in the best interests of the under-developed countries, but also to counter Soviet activities. It can be organized on a basis of mutual information and joint agreement. The nature of the co-operation, and the organizational forms it takes, will depend on the nature of the aid undertaken. The politico-economic activities of the Soviet Bloc countries should be closely watched and reported on by those NATO organizations which have been created to counter such activities. Where purely economic organizations are concerned, whether European or international, the countries of the West should not only keep each other informed, but should vote and, if necessary, act together.

In general the following principles should be observed:

(*a*) Co-operation between the under-developed countries themselves is urgently necessary in addition to bilateral assistance not only to avoid errors, but also in order to ensure that their own economies shall obtain the greatest possible benefit from the aid afforded them.

(*b*) Western co-operation with the under-developed countries should not be determined by Soviet actions, but should proceed according to its own principles. A direct answer to particular Soviet measures may occasionally be necessary; for example, Soviet attempts to underbid reasonable offers. But this should be the exception rather than the rule.

(c) Aid to the under-developed countries should normally take the 'general economic' form in order to strengthen their economic potential; and only in exceptional cases, and at their own wish, should 'politico-economic' aid be granted.

(d) All measures to aid the under-developed countries should be carefully attuned to their particular characteristics.

(e) Aid to the under-developed countries should be a mutual process; i.e., these countries themselves should take steps to ensure stability and continuity.

(f) As healthy competition is an essential of a free economy it should also be allowed to operate where measures designed to aid the under-developed countries are concerned. At the same time the degree of co-ordination should be sufficient to prevent their appearing outwardly as a form of market competition.

(g) The West should certainly counter direct Soviet political actions through its own political organizations. Economic aid for the under-developed countries should, generally speaking, be granted through the existing European and international economic organizations.

The Federal Republic has an important part to play in the bilateral assistance for those under-developed countries whose goodwill it enjoys. This goodwill is not merely due to the absence of any compromising colonial past, but also to an appreciation of German economic, technological and organizational skills. The participation of the Federal Republic is welcomed as assistance from a friend with the know-how.

The work of reconstruction which made the Federal Republic into one of the leading industrial nations of Europe was closely watched by the young countries of Asia and Africa. Now that this work is completed they are hoping that it will take an active part in their own economic development.

The Federal Republic will certainly do all it can to assist them, but as frankness is a necessary condition for any true partnership, one or two points must not be overlooked. First of all, the destruction caused by two world wars has resulted in a great shortage of capital in Germany. Further, Germany's economy is fully occupied, and

121

there is a shortage of technical and economic executives. All this means that our possibilities of aiding the under-developed countries are limited. This situation must be made clear at once in order to forestall exaggerated hopes which could only lead, through no fault of our own, to disappointment, and thus have an unfavourable effect upon our co-operation with the under-developed countries.

If we are to avoid anything like this we must make the best possible use of what possibilities of aid actually do exist, and co-operate with the under-developed countries on a long-term basis. Economically speaking this means that we must make up our minds on our long-term trading objectives, and how best to attain them.

The under-developed countries offer obvious expansion reserves for our foreign trade, but their economic development will require capital goods on a large scale, and the financing of such investments will cause difficulties. Generally speaking, medium-term financing up to periods of five years will not involve any insuperable difficulties, thanks to such institutions as the Exports Credit Society, but the situation is different where long-term export financing is involved. Nevertheless, the requirements of the under-developed countries, and the competitive conditions prevailing there, thanks in particular to the economic offensive of the Soviet Bloc, inevitably involve the granting of long-term credits. The Soviet Bloc grants credits ranging from ten to twenty years at rates of interest from two to two and a half per cent. And Western countries grant regular credits from six to ten years. As the necessary credits cannot be arranged in the Federal Republic either through the Note Bank or the ordinary commercial banks, various proposals are being considered to meet the case, such as the founding of a special bank, the re-establishment of the Gold Discount Bank, and so on.

Another way in which the economic development of these countries could be assisted is by the mobilization of their own native capital, and in this connection it should be remembered that the disinclination of native investors to take industrial risks, including the danger of sequestration, is likely to be reduced if native capital sees an opportunity of working together with foreign capital. Thus foreign capital flowing into under-developed countries can act as a sort of catalyst for economic development by helping to mobilize existing native capital otherwise lying idle. The necessary finance companies already exist in various countries.

On the whole the opportunities for assisting under-developed

122

countries by providing German capital are relatively few – at least by comparison with the desire and requirements of these countries. A German contribution to 'technological aid' can therefore be all the more important. Technological aid covers any contribution to the increase of technical know-how in the broadest sense. It can take the form of sending out technical experts, or inviting trainees to the Federal Republic by awarding scholarships and so on. The Federal Republic actually adopted a programme of this kind about three years ago, sending economic experts into the under-developed countries, and giving hospitality to trainees and scholarship-holders here, but it was a very restricted one.

In the meantime the Federal Parliament has voted a sum of fifty million marks for the year 1956–7 for the purposes of lending aid to the under-developed countries, and to consolidate our relations with them. This fund is to be used to increase their prosperity by systematically and permanently developing their resources. It is certainly not to be used for any unrealistic undertakings beyond the given stage of development of the countries in question, or even for undertakings which must operate on a normal economic basis if they are to contribute to the general prosperity of such countries. Generally speaking, the fund is to be applied to educational tasks in the broadest sense, with special reference to training in systematic economic activity.

Such operations can take on many and various forms; for example, the founding of technical training institutes, the holding of apprentice training courses, the running of model agricultural undertakings, experimental undertakings for the working up of native produce, hospitals, clinics, grants for students from under-developed countries to study technical, economic and managerial problems and so on, in the Federal Republic, courses for apprentices and others in German factories, discussions and planning by official experts or by German undertakings to be chosen by the Government of the country concerned, and the sending of experts in all forms of economic activity to the under-developed countries.

This wide programme of 'technological aid' will benefit both our economic and cultural co-operation with the under-developed countries. The fund is to be used not only for impressive projects aimed directly at furthering economic development and making our co-operation with these countries closer and more fruitful, but also for numerous smaller projects provided that they serve the general

123

aim. So far larger projects of this nature are a technical training institute in India and a model farm in Turkey.

In accordance with our view of a true partnership the individual projects are to be carried out as far as possible as joint undertakings of the Federal Republic and the countries concerned. In the ordinary way this would mean – for example with regard to the establishment of a technical training institute – that the Federal Government would provide the technical equipment and the training personnel, while the partner Government would provide the land and perhaps the buildings.

This co-operation on a government level would be supplemented by individual contacts in the personal sphere and by private organizations. Economic developments should take place – as, indeed, they are largely doing already – at a non-government level, and they should be made a matter of mutual enlightened self-interest. If we succeed in doing this then our activity will not only be more successful but less costly, and be purged of all taint of power politics. The technological aid programme can also be most effectively supported by private undertakings and private organizations.

It is therefore particularly desirable that mutual understanding and confidence should be encouraged by influencing public opinion both in the Federal Republic and in the under-developed countries.

To sum up: co-operation with the under-developed countries is one of the great tasks of our day, and it can be of long-term importance for future political and economic developments. The future position of the West in the world will depend on whether it can summon up the necessary ability and willingness to adopt constructive ideas, and the necessary understanding for new situations. The West should counter the advantages inherent in the political homogeneity of the Soviet Bloc by establishing mutual respect and understanding and adopting a uniform approach, and acting on jointly held principles. Western measures should not be restricted to independent political, economic and educational projects, or even to individual national programmes, but should represent an international whole.

The West should counter the methods of the Soviet Bloc with its own ideas, and it will have to demonstrate that its own economic and social system is sufficiently strong and vigorous to frustrate the political aims of that Bloc.

The Federal Republic regards co-operation with the under-developed countries as a true partnership working in joint responsibility for solutions appropriate to the given situation.

The West will have a future in the world only if it shows itself capable of fulfilling the tasks which now face it.

# 13

## Germany's Relationship to Eastern Europe*

FOR many centuries now there has probably been no generation which has not been troubled by the problem of Germany's relationship to Eastern Europe. In a confused and confusing time like the present I feel that a glance at history will make an interesting preface to my observations, particularly as the problem was never so urgent as it is today, and the conditions under which it can be settled were never so contradictory and so difficult to grasp. Post-war developments have taken us centuries back in history to prove with cogent reasons, or to dispute with less cogent ones, that Germany's frontiers do not lie on the Oder-Neisse Line; that the University of Königsberg at which Kant taught, and that Marienburg, which was the establishment of the Order of Teutonic Knights, are places whose return we may properly demand; that Silesia, the home of Angelus Silesius and Eichendorff, belongs to Germany's own cultural realm; and that the much-praised right of self-determination does not run contrary to the desires and hopes of all Germans that this territory should once again be united with Greater Germany.

But these historical considerations must not lead us to succumb to the dangerous temptation to draw comparisons from the historical relations of the German people to their Eastern European neighbours which would clash with present-day realities. Here too we might be tempted to preface our analysis of a complex of facts with considerations which would go beyond the limits of this lecture – for example, concerning the significance of history as a political science.

Do not misunderstand me: nothing is farther from my thoughts than to underestimate or deny the importance of a scientific historical

*Speech delivered at the University of Munich on January 18th 1957.

126

analysis. On the contrary, I feel that the German people in particular have every reason to occupy themselves constantly with historical happenings and to learn from the bitter but valuable experience of the past. A historical analysis such as I would desire as a statesman must be based on the realization that history is more than a sequence of events and dates, that it is not enough to examine past events according to their historical value or otherwise, and present causal relationships cogently. In my view when we regard history politically we should look at it as a sort of sociology of peoples and states. In other words, we should look at historical development in order to discover the roots of the disorder which has made the present picture so confusing. And we should remember and acknowledge that the relationship between governments and peoples is subject to the same unwritten laws that in the last resort determine the relationship between individuals.

In every stage of the sociological order the relationship of human beings to each other is determined by mutual acknowledgement, by respect for the individual, by the realization that the other man is different, and that we must live with him without his having to adapt his ideas and his behaviour to ours. The relationship of individuals to each other is determined by unwritten laws which are reflected in a system of law. This assumes in the last resort that individuals who live together, or who, as we say, have to get on with each other, recognize both these unwritten laws and the written laws, and let them control their attitude to each other. We may dispute as to whether such laws are inherent or based on ideas of natural law, so that their outer form is therefore an emanation of a natural order preceding States; or whether the order men have created for each other is based on a rational acceptance of restrictions on the right of one by the right of another, on the freedom of one by the freedom of another – the result in each case is the same: an adaptation to the generally recognized order is required, as well as the right to call to account whoever violates this order.

But let me return to my theme, and to what I said at the beginning, that it is dangerous to project historical events into the present. This is just what happens when one draws over-simplified comparisons and supposes that one can apply past comparisons with the present, since political facts and conditions will have changed. Ideas and considerations which may have determined Germany's policy towards Eastern Europe in the past are no longer valid today.

In the past century the face of Europe and the world was determined by the policy of so-called great powers: Great Britain, France and Russia. After the dissolution of the Holy Roman Empire, the Austro-Hungarian monarchy and Prussia, which was subsequently replaced by the German Empire of 1871, took their place in this circle of rising Great Powers, which determined world politics up to 1914. In the epoch before the First World War the United States was certainly a rising power, but in the world political game it was still an insignificant debtor country. It is therefore, I feel, an error to stand by Bismarck's alliance policy today, even though it was valuable and fruitful towards the end of the last century. The dynastic system of alliances which existed after the victory of the Allies over Napoleon had other roots and other aims, and it has no validity in our own day.

At the end of the First World War the whole world began to change. In the place of Tsarist Russia came Communist Russia, weakened by war, defeat and revolution. At the same time we saw the unprecedented rise of a new world power, the United States of America. The countries of the Far East, which up to then had been of interest chiefly to globe-trotters, art historians and writers, and perhaps businessmen, began to seek new paths, to grow independent and to attract the attention of the world both by the number of their inhabitants and by their evolutionary and revolutionary development.

Then came the Second World War, and its impact once again completely changed the world. We ourselves lived through this development. The European Great Powers, which thirty years previously had dominated world politics, now lost their preponderance. So much so that I think we must now recognize that not one of them is any longer in a position to determine its own future. It was, indeed, an irony of history that the deplorable pact between Hitler and Stalin created the conditions which led to the tremendous rise of the Soviet Union, the subjugation of the other East European peoples, and the extension of the political frontiers of the Soviet Union to the Elbe.

That is why when we talk about the relationship of Germany to Eastern Europe today we can no longer fall back on historical parallels. Neither the dismembered Germany of our own day, nor the reunited Germany of tomorrow, is or will be identical with the German Empire of 1871 or 1918 in the political relation of forces. What was perhaps permissible, and even right and necessary in the policy of the Weimar Republic towards Eastern Europe is no longer so

128

today. The balance of Great Powers has changed and political aims have changed with it. In 1917 it was possible to believe that it was clever and even right to undermine Russia in a critical phase of the First World War by sending Lenin in a sealed carriage from Switzerland to Russia. In the period after the First World War it was possible to believe that it was right and necessary to lead Germany out of her political and economic isolation by the policy of the Rapallo Pact. I do not want to discuss the relative value of these decisions today, but merely to point out that the conditions under which they were taken no longer exist. Germany's relationship to Eastern Europe must be recast, and this must be done on the basis of the realities of present-day political life. It doesn't help us to deplore them or rack our brains to find out to what extent Germany contributed to bringing them about.

Let me therefore now turn to the practical question of what policy Germany can and should pursue in relation to Eastern Europe today.

A new world has grown up there, and its content, its form and its political and social order are all strange to us. They are determined by a dialectical materialism which is said to have its roots in the teachings of Marx.

This world is strange to us and we reject its forms, and its social, economic and political order – or what passes for order, because it does not accord with our ideas of order – and we are not prepared to allow it entry into our own. I think this requires no proof. Germany is a country which is firmly rooted in the civilized world, and a free, democratic and lawful system of government is a matter of course. Let there be no misunderstanding on this point; all speculations that the German people might turn their backs on this order are pointless. Should the Soviet Union perhaps suppose that in our struggle for reunification we shall ever be prepared to abandon our freedom to gain that end it must be warned clearly and definitely against harbouring any such hopes.

But even to say this involves a temptation, and therefore a few words, not of justification but of explanation, are necessary because now and again, even in Germany, one gets the impression that the ideas of which I have spoken are misused, or at least devalued in discussion. We often talk of freedom, but even before this audience I cannot but wonder whether we are all truly aware what this word means to men in its deepest significance. However, I will resist the temptation to explain my own ideas of freedom, and content myself

E

with saying that those who passionately defend freedom as the most precious possession of man, mean freedom in its reciprocal relationship with discipline. There is no such thing as absolute freedom. Whoever claims that there is is consciously or unconsciously recommending anarchy. He is confusing freedom from intolerable restraint with freedom to intolerable action. He does not recognize, or refuses to recognize, that the freedom of man ends where the freedom of his fellow man begins. I have already said that in my view the relationship between peoples should accord at some point with that between men.

The German people have every reason to know what it means to talk about freedom and to live in freedom. In our past a totalitarian State did not merely restrict freedom, it abolished it altogether; the impersonal State adopted the amoral principle that what served the State was good – a horrible and absolutely perverted confusion.

I hardly think that it is necessary to say any more here than I have already said. In its most difficult times, in which economic distress was the background to despair and resignation the German people still showed that they were not prone to communist ideas.

There were times in which it seemed possible to evade such influences from the outside world by isolating ourselves. The Chinese Wall is a classic example of the way in which peoples sometimes sought to cut themselves off from the outside world. Such a wall serves not only to prevent him who is outside from entering, but it also curtails the perspective of him who lives within. Our present-day world has become too small for such mechanical means of isolation. The means of communication that span the world today are more powerful than those which existed in the past for a small village in the wilderness. We no longer communicate with each other by smoke signals or messengers, but by aeroplane and wireless.

Men and peoples live in a larger environment, one which is relatively easy to survey, but perhaps very difficult to understand. What we see in the world around us has to be taken into consideration in our political ideas. It would be altogether foolish and impractical – indeed, a policy of despair – to deny realities merely because they don't suit us.

This consideration must also determine our relationship with Eastern Europe today. I say this to forestall the foolish suggestion that the Federal Republic has ever thrust its head into the sand and refused to recognize the reality of States and forms of State merely because they happen not to fit in with its own outlook and its own desires.

Today Germany is once again between the West and the East. Formerly this was purely the result of her geographical position; today it is also the result of world political developments. One may welcome or deplore the fact that our world is lined up in power blocs, but the fact must be recognized and we must act accordingly, no matter how much we may hope that the tension which has produced this situation will one day disappear.

Thus Germany's position towards the rest of the world is clearly defined. I say Germany quite deliberately, and I am thinking not only of the Germany of today, but of the Germany of tomorrow as well. Germany is once and for all an integral part of that world which shares the same ideas and upholds the same ideals. For this world the words freedom, democracy, human dignity and law have the same meaning, even though in everyday life there may be differences. Each country that belongs to this particular world strives to arrange its inner order in accordance with its own ideas, but there is no essential difference between the economic, social and political order which might exist in the United Kingdom under a Conservative Government, that which might exist in the French Republic under a Socialist Government, and that which might exist in the United States under a Republican President. Their tax laws may be different, different views may be current concerning social security, but the values of which I spoke have the same validity in all these countries.

The totalitarian system of Communism with its ruthless suppression of personal freedom and its enslavement of man no more suits us than the arbitrary system which replaces law in all countries under its domination, and we deplore its contempt for those ideas which are sacred and inviolable for us.

Nevertheless, we, like others, are prepared to maintain relationships with such countries, and to discuss political, economic and cultural questions with them as far as the circumstances allow. However, no one should suppose that the establishment of such relationships is equivalent to the solution of existing problems; at the utmost it can facilitate a solution. It is therefore quite clear that such relationships are of a different character to the friendly ties we maintain with the countries of our own world.

With this I come to the central problem I propose to discuss; namely, our relations with the Soviet Union. For the moment I

131

propose to exclude the question of our relations with the other, so-called satellite, States in the Soviet orbit, and treat of them later in a different connection. Political realities have demonstrated that these States are not free and independent, but willy-nilly part of a block which is centrally controlled, and in which the individual has no greater independence as against the State than the individual State has as against the central power wielded from the Kremlin.

It is absolutely necessary that Germany should regulate her relationship to this part of the world in some way or other because she shares a common frontier with it, just as the Germany of yesterday did and the Germany of tomorrow will. But our Germany is dismembered, and we know that this intolerable situation will end only when the Soviet Union is prepared to agree to a solution. Don't misunderstand me: I do not grant to the Soviet Union, or to any other country in the world, the right to refuse to allow the German people to determine their own internal and external order. Whoever does that encroaches on the freedom of another people, and can neither justify nor conceal it with any form of cogent argument. However, the collapse of the Third Reich created a situation which we must face even if we are not prepared to accept it. Only in part of our Fatherland have we recovered the right to settle our own affairs on our own responsibility. Seventeen million of our fellow countrymen are under a foreign power and still deprived of this right. They are subject to a foreign will which is imposed upon them with the aid of certain wretched creatures of whom it is impossible to say whether they are more afraid of the Soviet Government or of their fellow Germans. Both in any case regard them with the utmost contempt. The Soviet Government needs them as pawns in its political game, and it well knows that their influence on this part of Germany derives not from their fellow countrymen, but from the power of the Soviet Union. All Germans on both sides of the zonal frontier are waiting and longing for the moment when they can use the lawful weapon of the free vote to rid themselves of such rulers.

We have established relations with the Soviet Union because we realize that the German problem, which burdens the whole world, no matter whether you regard it as cause, expression or consequence of international political tension, can be settled only when the Soviet Union is prepared to allow the German people a minimum of self-determination. In the circumstances the relation cannot be one of confidence, and certainly not of friendship. Normal relations between the German and Russian peoples will be possible only when the intolerable anomaly that the Soviet Union still insists on maintaining is finally removed. Nevertheless we do not doubt for one moment that the agreement we came to eighteen months ago in Moscow, and which was unanimously approved by the German Federal parliament, was right and necessary. Only that part of the German people which is free can speak for the whole. We alone can help to persuade the Soviet Union that the German people desire nothing which is inequitable when they demand their reunification in freedom. We are asking for no more and no less than other peoples, including the Russians, also claim for themselves. Only when this fateful question has finally been settled will it be possible to regulate our relationship to Eastern Europe anew. I am convinced that it will, in fact, be possible to persuade the Soviet Union that its own interests are reconcilable with the just claim of the German people – even more, that its own peaceable and steady development depends just as much on the solution of this problem as that of Germany does.

But we also know very well that the German people have neither the strength nor the opportunity to attain their objective on their own. For this we need the unfailing support of the whole free world; and as one who in recent years has borne part of the political responsibility I can say that we have already gained a very great deal in this respect.

Today we can say that the whole free world not only shows understanding for our claim but is prepared to support it. Those countries with which we have concluded a system of alliances have solemnly declared their intention of working with us for reunification; and they have further declared that they regard reunification as a plank in their own policy. This represents a declaration of solidarity by the free world with a people wishing to be free, a people whose moral and political value it would be difficult to over-estimate. And this political and moral support is not confined to a part of the free world. We are opposed at present only by Moscow and the Soviet Bloc it controls, while all other countries, no matter whether they are formally allied with us or not, have shown us their sympathy and support. The most convincing proof of this is the fact that no country in the free world – and here, of course, I include the non-committed countries – has accepted the Soviet thesis of two German States. Not one of these countries – from Japan to Indonesia, India and Pakistan, from the Arabian countries to North and South America and Australia – has recognized the so-called German Democratic Republic. All these countries, and there are almost ninety of them, recognize the German Federal Republic as the sole representative of the German people.

I do not propose to go into all the details of the problem of reunification here, but merely to say that all of us in Germany are agreed as to the aim even though we occasionally disagree as to the means of attaining it. No one in Germany questions the indissoluble association of a free Germany with the free world. Both the Government and the Opposition demand with equal emphasis that Germany must be free in the truest sense of the word and that this freedom must be guaranteed. And there is certainly no one in this audience who doubts for one moment that this is also the wish of the seventeen million Germans on the other side of the zonal frontier. If there is anyone anywhere in the world who doubts it then there is a simple way of settling the question. The day on which all seventy million Germans are allowed to determine their fate in a free vote will convince everyone that these seventy millions – apart perhaps from an infinitesimal minority impossible to define as a percentage – want the reunification of Germany in a free and democratic society based on law, a State which wishes to belong to the free world without in any way seeking hostility towards other nations which choose a different way of life.

This is what determines the relationship of present-day Germany to the countries of the Soviet Bloc and will similarly determine that of the Germany of tomorrow. We have not yet recognized the other States of the Soviet Bloc and we have no diplomatic relations with them. This does not mean that we deny their existence, or their right to exist. Our attitude to these countries is determined by the fact that there can be only one Germany. Whoever recognizes two German States, whoever accepts the dismemberment of Germany, violates the principle of self-determination. If we acted any differently we should compromise our own future and the moral and lawful demand of the German people for reunification in freedom. The whole world must be told that there is only one Germany, and only one German Government representing a free German people. Today that Government is the Federal Government, tomorrow it will be the Government of a reunited Germany holding its mandate from the free vote of the whole German people.

I feel that the events of the past few months have shown convincingly that we are on the right path. We know that the desire for freedom in the still unfree part of Germany has not perished. June 17th 1953 showed it unmistakably to the whole world. And the cowardly fear of free elections is convincing evidence that the men in Pankow know very well what the German people in the Soviet Zone are thinking.

But even in other parts of the Soviet empire the spirit of freedom is not dead. We have all seen the developments in Poland. No one knows how things there are going to develop, but at least we all know that last October the Polish people passionately demanded at least a minimum of freedom, and not all the show trials and the brutalities were able to prevent them. The Hungarian people have also given those who in their smug self-satisfaction no longer know what freedom is an example which fills us with deep emotion and enormous respect. The world had supposed that the word freedom had lost its meaning in these satellite States. It had thought that it was possible to brainwash people in such a way that they would passively consent to all that happened to them, but the happenings in Hungary have shown that even the most ruthless terrorism cannot uproot the longing for freedom. It is a blatant lie to pretend that reactionary clerico-fascist elements provoked a hopeless insurrection in the hope of robbing the Hungarian people of their achievements in the struggle against reaction and capitalism. Innumerable purges – as these measures are called – long ago wiped out such elements there and elsewhere, and in Hungary it was the young people, young workers and young students who were regarded as reliable enough to be given higher education, soldiers and officers of the Hungarian Red Army, and ordinary peasants who had been forced into collective farms, who rose against a government which had perpetuated itself for years by imprisoning, torturing and murdering its predecessors. Only the ruthless use of Soviet Russian troops and tanks was able to crush this revolution. Thousands lost their lives in the struggle for freedom, and thousands more fled from their country. None of us knows yet how things will develop in these two countries, but their peoples have called the attention of the whole world to their plight and canvassed its deepest sympathy. The United Nations is still discussing these events, and we observe with sadness and disappointment that though the conscience of the world was able to prevail in the Near East, where the intervention of the United Nations was accepted, this was not the case in Hungary because the Soviet Union and its satellites denounced it as an unjustifiable intervention in the affairs of a sovereign State. Nevertheless such noble discontent has arisen that it is out of the question that the Hungarian people will ever be willing to accept the situation even if they are unable to alter it.

Thus we see that developments have begun in the Soviet Bloc whose upshot none of us can foresee. We are not gratified by these events, since any such feeling would be an indefensible reaction to the tragedy, but at a meeting of the North Atlantic Community last December I did my best to explain what the German people are thinking about these things. We sincerely desire to put our relations with that part of the world in order. The unrest there is dangerous and tragic for us too. I have therefore put forward five principles to guide the relationship of the Federal Republic and the German people to these other peoples:

1. All peace-loving peoples should support the right of the peoples of Eastern Europe to self-determination and to choose their own governments in freedom;

2. The political order in the countries of Eastern Europe shall be based on the principles of national independence, national sovereignty, and the exclusion of all imperialist oppression;

3. These peoples must have the right to decide their social order in complete freedom;

4. Internal developments in these countries shall not be influenced by military force, by threats, or by political or economic pressure; and

5. No violation of the rights of man shall be tolerated in these countries.

How can we achieve this? I do not wish to repeat what I have already said so let me just point out that in the past the Federal Government has done everything in its power to uphold and consolidate the community of free peoples in the world and that it will continue to do so in the future through the proper organizations. In the past it was the Council of Europe, now it is also the North Atlantic Council and Western European Union. We have joined these communities not because we believe in a policy of force but because we are determined to resist it when it threatens us. Only a fool can deny that such a threat exists. The Soviet Union has advanced to the Elbe, and it refuses to grant the elementary rights of man to a section of the German people. The maintenance of this intolerable situation represents a constant threat, and the German people are not prepared to submit to it without resistance. They are prepared to defend their new-won freedom, but this is possible only together with all those others who accept the same principles.

We are told that a policy of force is wrong and dangerous, and I quite agree, but what responsible person in Germany thinks of adopting such a policy? Who is the aggressor? He who defends the right, or he who violates it? Who is threatening whom? Should we abolish the fire brigade in the hope that there will be no more fires? Or should we wait until measures have been taken to prevent fires? Our ideas of a just solution have been put to the Berlin Conference and to the Geneva conferences. I do not want to repeat our proposals here. So far every suggestion has been rejected by the Soviet Union. This is true of disarmament, which we earnestly desire and are determined to work for. It is also true of reunification, and of a security system which will allow everyone without exception to live in peace. When Germany and her allies called for free elections we were told that the German people were not yet ready for them. Later we were told that free elections were undemocratic; and finally that a reunited Germany would represent a danger to her neighbours in both the East and the West. When proposals were put forward in Geneva for a security and guarantee system which would forestall this alleged danger we were told that the German people in the Soviet Zone must not be robbed of the social achievements they were enjoying. Incidentally, we know just how much these so-called achievements are worth. When we claimed that no people should be denied the right to settle its own internal and external affairs we were told that the sovereign German Democratic Republic must be allowed to decide its own relationship to the rest of Germany; and direct negotiations between Berlin and Pankow were suggested. Although they know that such negotiations are impossible, and that if they did take place it would be between a free government on one hand and puppets on the other, who would merely mouth the instructions they had been given, the suggestion was repeated. When it was then proposed that Germany should be neutralized, this was also rejected as insufficient, with the argument that such a Germany, which would, of course, have no practical control over her decisions or actions, would have to accept the Russian form of Socialism and be incorporated in the Russian sphere of influence.

137

Germany is prepared to enter with her allies into any reasonable discussion with Eastern Europe. Neither the Federal Republic now, nor any reunited Germany in the future, will ever threaten anyone anywhere. The German people are in favour of real co-existence, and by this I mean a situation in which peoples with different political set-ups can live peacefully side by side. Co-existence is real only if it recognizes the right of each people to live its own life in its own way. The terrible example of co-existence as applied to Hungary is not attractive. That form of co-existence has meant that Mongols can become gunmen in Budapest while Hungarians are banished to Siberia.

When one talks of Germany's relationship to Eastern Europe, i.e., to the Soviet Union, one should not talk of the price we are prepared to pay for it. We are certainly prepared to make real sacrifices, but when we demand freedom we mean freedom whole and entire and not shackled with a mortgage we are expected to pay off as the price of freedom. And when we talk of freedom we mean freedom which is guaranteed and secure, since anything else is a dangerous illusion. If we are persistent and determined it will not be possible to deny us freedom indefinitely. The whole world, including the Soviet Union, recognizes that the arbitrary dismemberment of Germany is an anomaly which burdens the German people and makes their relationship to the Russian people intolerable. In fact, the whole world is suffering from the resultant tension. It is like a smouldering fire covered by a blanket. Tomorrow the flames may burst through after all. Let no one suppose that I am uttering a threat, I am merely expressing a very real anxiety. There is perhaps no other people who so earnestly desire peace as the German people do, for hardly any other people have experienced the horrors of war more than they have. We have not forgotten the millions of our fellow countrymen who were murdered in the concentration camps, who lost their lives or their nearest and dearest in the war, who lost their homes and their livelihoods by exploitation and bombing.

We have done everything in our power to place our relationship to the world around us on a new basis, and I am happy to feel that there was probably never a time in the past when we could say with equal truth that our relationship to the West was so clear and straightforward. Our enemies in the Second World War have become our friends and partners. They have helped us and they are still helping us, and they are joining their efforts to ours to bring permanent peace to the world. Let me cite two examples from the recent past. There is the agreement between Belgium and Germany, which settled all outstanding questions from the war years that compromised the relationship between the two countries, and restored an atmosphere of friendship and mutual goodwill. And even stronger is the agreement between France and Germany, by which the Saar was enabled to return to Germany. We should like to regulate our relationship to Eastern Europe in the same spirit, even though we know that our ideas, and even the moral basis of our way of life, would not permit the same procedure. But even where friendship is not yet possible, and where the moral basis of thought and action are so fundamentally different, there must be some way in which nations can live together to the benefit of all.

Where there is no agreement there must, above all, be tolerance, but tolerance in the true sense, tolerance in behaviour, not in ideas. Anything else would compromise essential principles. But true tolerance can be the basis of the political and moral relationship of Germany to Eastern Europe.

Allow me to close by quoting the concluding passage of the Government declaration of June 28th 1956:

> 'The Federal Government holds that the tragic conflict between might and right, whose victim is the German people, is the expression of a profound disorder in the world. It is our joint task to help might to use right in establishing a new and lasting order, but that right should also use might when right is in danger of being violated.'

# 14

# Germany's Relationship to India*

I AM particularly happy to be able to address the Indian Council of World Affairs and say a few words about the principles of German foreign policy, and also about the relations between the Indian and German peoples and their Governments.

I am thinking in particular of the speech your Premier Pandit Nehru made to the Society for Foreign Affairs in Bonn last year. Those of us who were privileged to hear it were deeply impressed by the eloquence and wisdom of your great statesman, who gave us a valuable insight into the complicated problems facing your country, and left us with a deep impression of energy and confidence in the future, which is also true, we feel, of the whole Indian people.

I am very glad that as a guest of the Indian Government I can bring you the greetings of the German people and express the sincere wish that in the future the relations between our two peoples will become even closer in all spheres of political, economic and intellectual life.

There have already been promising beginnings. Allow me to recall that a little while ago we had the pleasure of welcoming your Minister of Education, Maulana Azad, to Germany. Shortly after that our own Vice-Chancellor Blücher paid India a visit, and a few months later your Premier visited us. The discussions which began then were continued a few weeks ago when Pandit Nehru met our Chancellor, Doctor Adenauer, for a friendly exchange of views on returning from a trip to the United States and Canada.

All these visits, including my own, are of special importance against the background of the long-established relations between

*Speech delivered on March 28th 1957 during an official visit to India.

140

India and Germany, which go back into past centuries when German scholars and writers were privileged to co-operate in the rediscovery of your great past.

It is not only today that Germans are interested in Indology. German studies go back to the eighteenth century. It was in 1791 that the German traveller and explorer Georg Forster translated the 'Sakuntala' of Kalidasas, and thus awakened German interest in your language and your literature. The work was received in Germany with great enthusiasm and made a deep impression on poets and philosophers like Goethe and Herder.

German interest in India steadily increased and the study of Indian philosophy and philology extended rapidly. The beginnings of these studies lie even farther back, and it was in the seventeenth century that German scholars produced the first Sanscrit grammar. Others followed in the eighteenth and nineteenth centuries. The first Tamil grammar was published in Halle in 1716. Indology in Germany reached a new peak in the nineteenth century when Franz Bopp published the first work on Indo-Germanic language affinity, Schlegel and the brothers Humboldt made the spiritual heritage of India available to Germany – Friedrich Schlegel translated the 'Bhagavadgita' in 1823 – and Christian Lassen published the first encyclopaedia of Indian archaeology. Poets like Friedrich Rückert, historians like Albrecht Weber, and philosophers like Arthur Schopenhauer and Paul Deussen, were all inspired by India. I need only mention the name of Max Müller, a German who restored the treasures of Vedantic literature to India, and who was given, I am told, the Sanscrit name of Moksa Mula here.

These traditions are being upheld in our own day, and German Indology is represented by such men as Ludwig Alsdorf, Helmuth von Glasenapp and Helmut Hoffmann, who also enjoy a reputation in your country.

I will restrict myself to this short resumé of historical facts. They are certainly of importance for the development of our relations, which now have a new basis with the establishment of the free and independent State of India.

I think I can say that the German people in particular showed a deep understanding for and sincere sympathy with the desire of the Indian people for freedom, and I feel that there are certain parallels in the history of our two peoples. In both countries the consciousness of unity was an integral part in their strongest spiritual and cultural

141

forces. The great protagonists of freedom in your country, men like Mahatma Gandhi, Jawaharlal Nehru and Vallabhai Patel, were dominated by this idea, and their profound conviction of the spiritual and cultural unity of the Indian people gave them that tremendous *élan* which finally brought the great day of independence to India on August 15th 1947.

From the very first the relations between the independent Indian people and the German people were frank and friendly. We Germans have not forgotten that India was the first country which ended the state of war after the Second World War, and since then fruitful relations have been opened up on many fields. German firms and German technicians are taking part in the great task of building up modern India, and co-operating in the drawing up of your great plans for industrialization, which are being watched with interest and admiration everywhere. I will mention only the steelworks erected by German firms in Rourkela, perhaps the most outstanding example of Indo-German co-operation. All Indo-German discussions, whether in Delhi or in Bonn, have sought ways and means of increasing this co-operation, and I can assure you that so far as the Indian Government desires it we shall do our utmost to assist in the great work of raising Indian living standards.

However, I feel that Indo-German relations are based on other things beside historico-scientific and economic co-operation. In my view the most permanent basis of Indo-German friendship is a similarity of certain fundamental principles and aims. Let me mention what is perhaps the most significant thing: the joint conviction of our two peoples that our fate is ultimately determined not by material but spiritual and moral values. We live in an age in which materialism threatens to dominate man's existence as never before, an age in which technology and the striving for riches and power engulf the lives of peoples and individuals to an ever-increasing extent. Material goods are certainly a necessary condition of our life, but are not its content.

Both the Indian and the German people place the freedom of the individual and of the nation higher than all material goods. We are both equally convinced that democracy and the recognition of the rights of man are the things that make the life of man worth while. Only recently the German people have suffered bitterly under a dictatorship. It brought us all endless misfortune and plunged the world into a war that threatened our very existence as a people. We have not forgotten this experience and you may be sure that we shall never again allow a small group of irresponsible politicians to take power in our country. This determination is the basis of the German Federal Government's policy. Together with the whole German people, it is determined to do everything in its power to serve world freedom and consolidate world peace.

Let me speak of freedom first, because it is the most urgent concern of the German people. With their Potsdam decisions the victorious powers temporarily took over political responsibility for the German people. Even if they had not voluntarily agreed to do so it would, after a certain transitional period, have been their duty to hand back the right to self-determination and the duties of free responsibility to the German people. This has already been done in the greater part of my Fatherland. The United States, Great Britain and France have given sovereignty back to fifty million Germans in the territory of the Federal Republic. With this they gave us the opportunity of building up a new State on the principles of a free and legally based democracy. This new development began with the proclamation of the provisional Constitution and the holding of free elections in 1949, and today I can say with justifiable pride that it has borne fruit. The ceaseless efforts of the Federal Government have succeeded in bringing the free part of Germany back into the family of free peoples of the world as a respected member. It has re-established Germany's prestige, restored her good name, and won friends in all parts of the world. We knew that this was our most urgent task and we did not hesitate to make sacrifices for it.

But eighteen million Germans are unable to take any share in it. In that part of Germany which is occupied by the Soviet Union the basic rights and liberties of human beings have not been restored. The insistent and unswerving demand of the whole German people that their national unity should be restored in freedom has not yet been granted.

What the German people demand is not much, and certainly not too much. We want the same freedom and the same right of self-determination as other peoples rightly claim for themselves and which we shall always be prepared to grant them. We want the rights solemnly proclaimed in the United Nations Charter to apply to Germany too. The separation of Germany into a free and an unfree part is not based on the will of the German people. It came about against their will and it continues against their will. The German

143

people regard the perpetuation of this injustice as a permanent and unforgiveable violation of the written and unwritten laws which should govern the co-existence of peoples, as a continuous and inexcusable interference in matters which concern them alone.

The German people demand freedom in order to live in freedom, and not to misuse it, and therefore the efforts of the Federal Government are equally directed to the safeguarding of peace. We know that peace and freedom are indivisible. Where there is no freedom there is also no peace, and outward appearances make no difference. We are equally convinced that freedom can flourish only in peace, since in the last resort all violent conflicts not only disturb peace but represent a great encroachment on freedom.

The German people have suffered the terrible experience of a war unleashed by conscienceless politicians which plunged the whole world into chaos. Germans still remember the destruction of their towns, the deaths of millions of their fellow countrymen in battle and at home, and the fate of twelve millions who were driven from hearth and home. The German people know that peace is necessary if they are to continue their work of economic and social reconstruction.

For this reason there is nothing we more strongly desire than good neighbourly relations with all the countries on our frontiers and firm friendship with all the peoples of the world who cherish the same values that we cherish. Ideological differences should not, I feel, prevent understanding, co-existence and mutual assistance.

In one part of the European continent at least we have succeeded in bringing this about, and I am happy to feel that we have established a permanent understanding based on equal rights, friendship and mutual respect. One example of this is the relationship that now exists between France and Germany. In the past our relationship was disturbed by tension, and there were repeated bitter collisions; today we have succeeded in solving all our problems in a spirit of reconciliation, whose outward expression was the return of the Saar. This policy cleared the way for the European Coal and Steel Community, and for the Common Market and EURATOM, whose respective agreements have just been signed in Rome.

The participating States and in particular the Federal Republic have repeatedly and solemnly renounced any appeal to force. There are no differences between us and other countries that Germany considers settling with force. And when I say this I am thinking in particular of Eastern Europe. The German people equally desire a permanent peace with their eastern neighbours based on friendship and confidence. This is true also of our relationship with Poland. We all of us remember the unholy alliance between Hitler and Stalin in 1939 of which Poland was the victim. Poland too may rest assured that we recognize her vital rights and that we are awaiting the day when a free Germany will be able to talk to a free Poland and settle our mutual relations. The success of the Franco-German negotiations encourages me to believe that we should then succeed in finding a settlement in respect of the German territory which the Potsdam agreement placed under temporary Polish administration. In any case I solemnly declare that we are exclusively seeking a peaceable understanding and the peaceable co-existence of the two peoples, and in doing so I know that I have the support of the whole German people, both the Germans living in the Federal Republic and those in the Soviet Zone.

Allow me to repeat a declaration here that I made on behalf of the Federal Government last December:

1. All peace-loving peoples should lend their full support to the right of the East European peoples to self-determination and to choose their own governments in complete freedom;

2. The political order in the East European States should be based on the principles of national independence and sovereignty, and the abolition of all imperialist oppression;

3. All East European countries should have the right to choose their own social order in complete freedom;

4. Internal developments in these countries should not be influenced by military force, threats or economic pressure;

5. No violations of the rights of man in these countries should be tolerated.

The German people feel the same way about the Russian people. Bitter and ruthless warfare has done untold damage to both peoples. We look to the future and are prepared to do our utmost to prevent any repetition of such a disaster. At the same time we shall not cease to remind the Soviet Union of its political and moral obligation to allow the German people the rights it claims for itself. The reunification of my Fatherland must not take place by force. We therefore propose the peaceable and democratic method of free elections in the whole of Germany, both in the Federal Republic and in the Soviet Zone. The Federal Republic is fully prepared to accept the result of such elections. A freely-elected German parliament and a freely-elected German Government would then organize the economic and social order of a reunited Germany in accordance with the wishes of the German people, and represent Germany as a free partner in a peaceful world based on the principles laid down in the Charter of the United Nations. These were the principles agreed to between the Federal Government and your own Premier during his visit to Bonn in July last year. Your Premier and our Federal Chancellor were at one in the belief that the basis for friendly and peaceful co-operation between all peoples must be respect for national independence, national sovereignty, and territorial integrity, and non-interference in the internal affairs of other countries.

All the foreign political decisions of the Federal Government have been directed towards these high aims. I spoke of the passionate desire of the German people for peace and freedom, but we must remember that peace and freedom are possible only in stable conditions, and I will not conceal their present fear of aggression. In fact they regard the refusal of their right to reunite as a permanent act of aggression in violation of the principles of the United Nations Charter and the ideas of all peoples who are in favour of unrestricted freedom. I feel that particularly in your country we shall meet with sympathy and political understanding for our views. Germany has done her best to emerge from the deplorable isolation into which she was forced as a result of the last war. She is aware that she cannot exist on her own. Seventy million people have to live in a relatively restricted area. She has done everything possible to open her frontiers, and establish political and economic relations and friendships with the world around her, to some extent because she feels herself directly threatened. No one in Germany is thinking of aggression. The alliances Germany has entered into are exclusively defensive in character, and I feel that in so doing she has provided the best guarantee for a continuation of her policy of peace.

We may deplore the fact that the world seems to be divided into blocs which regard each other with mutual suspicion, but Germany was not responsible for this development and she has merely drawn the unavoidable conclusions from a situation she regrets. However, there are ways in which this intolerable tension can be removed from the world.

Everywhere people conscious of their responsibility are working persistently to achieve world-wide disarmament. Germany will always support efforts to persuade all countries to pledge themselves to disarmament and effective and unrestricted control.

However, it would be a dangerous illusion to suppose that any permanent peace could rest safely on facts which themselves represent a constant threat to peace. This is true in particular of the dismemberment of Germany. Only a reunited Germany could be an effective partner to a disarmament agreement and the abolition of the intolerable tension which at present threatens the world. Such a Germany would be prepared at any time to give other peoples every possible guarantee of security, and to join in an effective security system, provided that her own freedom of political action were not restricted beyond the general obligations arrived at by joint and mutual agreements. The German people cannot be reproached for declaring themselves clearly and definitely in favour of the free world, or for wishing that their friendly relations with those parts of the world with which they feel themselves deeply associated shall not be disturbed.

Let me stress once again the great importance of those agreements which have led to the formation of the European Coal and Steel Community, the Common Market and EURATOM. By taking part in these agreements Germany has voluntarily joined a larger community which desires peace and pledges itself to freedom, which seeks to increase the well-being of its peoples, to give men and women a feeling of security, and to seek their greatest possible happiness in the given circumstances. The German people will remain loyal to these aims, and they look to all other peoples for support.

# 15

## Cultural Problems of Foreign Policy*

FIRST of all I should like to thank you, Prime Minister, and the Association of Christian-Social Academicians for the opportunity to address you on a subject that interests us all, and should interest us in particular because it is not directly connected with everyday political matters. I feel that it would not be appropriate either to the place or my audience if I restricted myself to giving you a report on the cultural activities of the Foreign Office. I certainly do not propose to avoid discussing these activities, but I feel that I will be meeting your wishes if I also discuss the ideas which lie behind our cultural policy abroad. Such a discussion of general principles is all the more important because any cultural foreign policy not based in principle on our membership of Western civilization would degenerate into opportunism.

The expression cultural policy did not arise at all until about forty or fifty years ago, but if we leave aside the suggestion that it is something consciously directed beyond our own frontiers, then certainly the idea is much older. Great princes and lesser ones, cities and republics, in short, civilized communities in general, have always striven to establish a connection between politics and cultural affairs. Art and literature were encouraged, books and pictures were collected, sacred and profane buildings were erected, universities, academies, schools and theatres were founded. In fact certain artistic, scientific and educational endeavours would be impossible without the support, even the guidance, of the State.

There is nothing out of the ordinary in this co-operation between

*Speech to the Association of Christian-Social Academicians on January 16th 1958 at Munich University.

148

the State and culture. Leaving aside the question of whether the State in Jakob Burckhardt's interpretation is, as a work of art itself, part and parcel of our culture, politics and culture still have common roots and common aims.

We all know that the word 'culture' comes from the Latin *'colere'* and indicates cultivation and tillage, an activity such as agriculture; and the idea it expresses is that with his hands and his brain man turns unregulated nature into something ordered and regulated. Culture is opposed to chaos and barbarism. It strives to establish order and gain the benefits of order – and this extends perhaps from agriculture to those spiritual uplands where, to quote Hölderlin, God's lightning flashes.

The word 'politics' also goes far back into the antique past, to the Greek *polis*, to the City State, which liked to think of itself as the embodiment of 'fair order', as the Cosmos. Politics are nothing but an effort to regulate society in the State and the community of States, the effort to master the art of ordered and moral living together. Here too, therefore, the idea of order plays the decisive role. Politics and culture are related to the extent that they have the same aim; namely, order. It is just that politics as the ordering of society, as the public facet of the effort for order, assumes culture as the effort of the individual for order, since where there is no longer any vital culture, politics verges on barbarism – as we have good cause to know.

At the same time there is a certain mutual tension between politics and culture. Although they both strive towards order they differ in their attitude and their operation. The State must impose order, if necessary by force, but culture can exist only in a condition of freedom, and, in particular, the freedom of the creative individual. The widely deplored extension of the power of the modern State is therefore not favourable to culture, and an excess of State power and authority can prove fatal to it.

In such circumstances cultural policy can then lead to abuse and perversion. In a dictatorship the cultural spheres lose their independence. The State becomes the supreme judge of the work of art: it approves or disapproves from a political and propaganda angle. Cultural achievements are then directed towards a totalitarian State order. Nothing but glorification of the totalitarian system is allowed, and cultural policy directed beyond the frontiers is nothing but the handmaid of the State. But where the State, or the all-powerful party, regulates what may be done and how it may be done, and refuses to allow the proper presentation of any real conflict, where the formal development of a work of art is subject to the judgement of official-dom, where there is no longer any free and independent science striving for objectivity, real culture can no longer flourish. In such circumstances art is reduced to the wretched productions of a devitalized naturalism and a cheap party and personality cult such as Hitler loved and such as fills the modern rooms of the Tretyakov Gallery in Moscow. In architecture you have the bombastic and pompous buildings erected during the Third Reich, and those extraordinary monumental piles to be seen in the towns and cities of the Soviet Union, and in Stalin Avenue in East Berlin. You also have that pseudo-science which is fundamentally nothing but political propaganda because it no longer represents a search for truth in freedom. I could give you such examples *ad libitum*. Perhaps there are spheres which are not open to political tendencies, or at least ought not to be open. But even there you find encroachments – music and the natural sciences, for example, or the attitude of Soviet science in the question of genetics. And what a price has to be paid for really outstanding technical achievements under a totalitarian system! They are purchased at the expense of the highest achievement of human culture; namely, the freedom of the individual to be himself and call the fruits of his labour his own.

The basic principles of subordination and solidarity which must guide true politics must also be those of any true cultural policy. Culture is properly a matter of the individual and of the smaller group. And where the individual and the smaller group can no longer manage alone then the next larger group or higher group must be brought in to help, if help is at all possible, since it is a matter of course that no great cultural achievement, whether literary, musical or otherwise, can be produced or enforced by the State. In other words, true cultural policy should strive to make itself unnecessary. I am certainly not saying this in order to excuse any failing on the part of the State to encourage culture. When I think of the present situation in education, and particularly higher education, in the health services and in scientific research, then – without forgetting that in the past other tasks have perhaps been more urgent – I cannot help feeling that the State does not do enough in Germany today. And the same is true of our official cultural activities abroad.

It is in any case the task of the State to do everything possible to make cultural values available to all, to release and further cultural tendencies. The State itself as a political institution expressing itself in various forms, as a government, as a civil service, as a parliament, cannot invent, cannot produce works of literature and works of art, cannot compose music, but it can help to create the conditions in which individuals can do these things.

Nowadays cultural policy beyond the frontiers plays an important and very proper part in the general policy of all States. Properly conceived it has two tasks: to set out its own achievement and to co-operate internationally.

Culture operates in its own circles, and there are national differences that cannot and should not be effaced or flattened out, since they contribute in particular to that rich and many-sided thing we call human culture. Paul Valéry once said: 'Let us enrich ourselves on the differences between us.' Nevertheless, it would be unnatural if we did not feel the urge to communicate our own to other peoples, to show them the riches and achievements of our own national culture, because the relationship between States and between peoples corresponds to a certain extent to the relationship between individuals. Cultural achievements can enhance the prestige of a State even though its political prestige has declined – perhaps a point of particular importance for us. Cultural policy – if I may be allowed to use such an expression – should not serve politics by lies and boasting, and it should certainly not be at the expense of the guest country. It should aim at correcting errors, dissipating prejudice, and creating understanding and confidence.

Unless spiritual and cultural life is prepared to see itself crippled it must not isolate itself, for that would be the end of its own development. It needs mutual understanding, mutual exchange and communication. The greatest achievements of culture arise out of the mutual play of giving and taking. Think, for example, of Gothic architecture, the medieval epic, the Renaissance, Baroque art, and classic and romantic literature in Germany – none of them would be conceivable without communication with French, Spanish, Italian and English minds. German culture stagnated during the period of National Socialist autarky, arrogance and racial obscurantism. A cultural foreign policy must aim at international exchange, and this also means that it must strive to awaken appreciation at home for the achievements of other countries. And I do feel that as Germans we can look back on a good tradition in this respect. German scholars, philologists, geographers, art historians and religious historians were in the van in making the spiritual treasures of India, China, Islam and Buddhism known not only to the German people but to the world at large. This accounts to a great extent for the sympathy which Germany enjoys in Asia today. In this connection I recall in particular the interest shown during my visit to India in Germany's Sanscrit scholars, whose names mean something in Indian intellectual life today. The sphere of such a foreign cultural policy is very broad and many-sided. Specific activities are concerned with science and education. There is an exchange of scholars, teachers and students by means of scholarships, grants and lecture tours. Then there is the exchange of publications, the founding of schools abroad, language courses, the exchange and translation of books, book exhibitions, and so on. In addition there is the organization of art exhibitions, tours by operatic and dramatic companies, orchestras and individual artists, the sending of films and records. Very important too is the establishment and maintenance of various cultural institutes. During my travels in many parts of the world the value of scientific institutes, libraries and reading-rooms has been particularly borne in on me. Bilateral cultural relations can be regulated by cultural agreements, whilst multilateral organizations can ensure co-operation in a still wider sphere.

Various countries use various methods, and they are all worthy of our attention. There are two extremes here which both come in for a good deal of discussion. One is to exclude any element of politics as far as possible, or at least to prevent its being obvious. The matter is then left largely in the hands of cultural organizations as such, and the countries who prefer this method do not maintain a cultural department in their Foreign Office as we do. This is the method Great Britain adopts, and it is served by that excellent institution the British Council, which maintains no less than 120 English libraries abroad. Those who are in favour of this approach feel that it leaves cultural affairs independent, and reduces the possibility of inexpert official intervention to a minimum, and that the less the Government and politics have to do with cultural policy abroad the better – and I for one would hesitate to deny it.

The other method works through official channels, cultural departments attached to the Foreign Offices, and official cultural representatives abroad, such as we know on the continent and in our own country. Here, of course, the influence of the Government is more obvious, but this, too, has certain advantages. I do not propose to go into the matter in detail, but an argument whose cogency impresses me is that our representative institutions abroad are best able to judge what is needed and what is likely to be willingly accepted – provided, of course, that we have the right men on the job. Since both methods have their advantages I think it is a good idea to combine them, and that is what we do. In addition to the cultural activities of our Foreign Office abroad, there is the German Academic Exchange Service, the Goethe Institute here in Munich, the Institute for Foreign Relations in Stuttgart, the Inter Nationes in Bonn, the German Research Association, the documentary and information service of the Religious Ministerial Conference, and a department for cultural affairs attached to the Ministry of the Interior. Without going any further into the matter I think I can truly say that nowadays there is really no cause for misgiving about the methods of our cultural policy abroad.

But irrespective of which methods are given preference the main thing is to find the right men to shoulder the responsibility for this aspect of our foreign policy both at home and abroad. We need not only writers, artists, musicians and scientists, but also men who know foreign countries, understand their peoples, do their best to appreciate their particular characteristics, and have some knowledge of what is required and what is expected of us. Ideas on the subject are very varied, and it is not at all easy to find men and women who are capable of carrying out these particular tasks, who have the necessary flair and the requisite intimate relationship to cultural matters.

Allow me to say a few words about the general situation in which these activities have to be conducted. In order to understand it we must not overlook its particular difficulties.

First of all we must recognize regretfully that the policy previously pursued in this respect was barren. During the years of National Socialism, war and the subsequent collapse, German schools and institutes abroad were all closed down and most of their buildings confiscated. German language courses ceased and so did scientific exchange. For many years Germany was just not culturally represented at all in many important countries. Knowledge of the German language which had always been an academic instrument of great value in many countries greatly declined, particularly amongst the younger generations. Many countries reorganized their foreign cultural relations.

But much worse than all this was the fact that owing to the

153

deplorable developments in our country from 1933 on we lost that confidence in us that we had previously enjoyed in cultural matters abroad. Respect for German culture still exists abroad, and its historical achievements are not disputed, but the methods adopted by the Third Reich created mistrust and an instinctive rejection of all forms of German cultural activity. Our first task is to dissipate this resentment, which still exists in many places. But even where there is still, or again, confidence, there is a tendency which fills me with anxiety; namely, the idea that although our scientific and technological achievements are worthy of admiration, and our present political leadership worthy of confidence, the present-day cultural achievements of the German people are not worth consideration.

What I have said about the difficulties abroad matches developments at home. First of all there was the break in the continuity of our own cultural life, and this naturally particularly affects the younger generation. We are faced with a situation in which our cultural heritage is respected but regarded as something of which we have no direct knowledge, something that interested people have to bestir themselves to acquire, something which is only a memory and provides no direct impulse for our cultural life today. We hesitate to attach ourselves to this past cultural tradition, perhaps because we have not yet altogether made up our minds about what now lies behind us, and because many of us are only too anxious to efface all psychological and spiritual traces of it from our memory, or to dismiss it altogether as an historical accident in our development.

This is obviously the reason why our economic recovery, which is so often and so wrongly described as 'an economic miracle', has not been accompanied by any corresponding 'cultural miracle'. Unfortunately we must admit that our economic and technological achievements are not matched by corresponding achievements in our scientific and cultural life. Culture must, of course, grow on its own, and we could all produce various reasons to explain why the surprising cultural resurgence which took place after the First World War found no parallel after the Second. The German people lost valuable talent by death, destruction and emigration, and, in addition, they were under enormous spiritual pressure and had to fight desperately to exist at all. But let us not attempt to deny that the enforced obsession with everyday matters, and the fear for the morrow, which resulted from our post-war miseries, has led to an excessively materialistic outlook which leaves little room for the things of the mind. At the same time we should be evading our responsibilities if we merely accepted this state of affairs.

Here and there we can see evidence of dissatisfaction with it, and this could be the first step to an improvement; but, of course, it is far from being general, and this raises a further question – it is no more than that: do we now lack that desire for cultural achievement which was once a specific characteristic of Germans? There were times in our history, let me recall, when our relationship to cultural affairs was almost religious.

It isn't that our people are hostile to culture today; it is just that they have become indifferent to it, and regard it as no more than something decorative, as a luxury. Perhaps there is food for thought for us in the observation that in other countries so very many men have entered into political life from the world of culture. I am thinking of men like Giraudoux, Paul Claudel and François Poncet. Fortunately we are not entirely out of it in this respect, and I recall with pleasure that our first post-war ambassador to Paris was Wilhelm Hausenstein, a man of your own city.

There is something else we should think over. Isn't it unfortunately true that we tend to neglect the moral sciences? I do not deny that in a world in which technology plays such a big role we certainly need scientists as such, and that we must perhaps even allow them precedence. But don't we also need men whose minds go beyond the sphere of technology? Men who remind us that nuclear physics are not the most important thing in life, and that only the humanities and the spirit that goes with them can hold it in proper bounds? Perhaps here is one of the greatest tasks of cultural policy, not only in Germany but in all other countries.

In this respect I should like to quote a letter written by Chancellor Bethmann-Hollweg in 1913. Referring specifically to this question of cultural representation abroad he says:

'What France and England are doing in this sphere is not the achievement of their Governments alone, but of the nations as a whole, of the unity and homogeneity of their civilization, the purposeful assertion of the nations as such. We have not got that far. We are not sufficiently conscious and confident of our own culture, of our own national being and national ideals. We are a young people, and perhaps we are too much imbued with a naïve belief in might. We underestimate more sophisticated methods, and we do not yet realize that what might can attain can never be retained by might alone.'

I feel that these observations made in 1913 have lost none of their validity today. But what is the valid expression of German culture?

What can we do to create a valid image of ourselves abroad? It is not an easy question to answer and I hope you will not expect a generally applicable definition from me, but at least I will try to get nearer to an answer by a process of elimination.

The theme chosen by an author or an artist is certainly not the main thing, nor is the so-called national attitude. It is only in totalitarian States, which have no real relationship to culture anyway, that they first want to see a man's party card before deciding whether he's an artist or not. The determining factor must always be artistic or scientific quality. Perhaps this explains why we have so far not been represented by modern films, for example, at international film festivals such as France and Italy have organized with great success.

On the other hand, we must not overlook, or attempt to deny, the fact that politics is a whole: an acknowledgement of absolute values, an acknowledgement of moral ideas. It is a false idea of objectivity for a State to encourage those who declare themselves morally neutral and who mock and resent any appeal to moral principles in public life. Respect for the dignity of man and the upholding of that freedom and justice which is rooted in Christianity forms the basis of our civilization, and they should, I feel, also form the basis of our politics. In my view they belong to the inalienable essence of political thought and action, which I for one would not be prepared to abandon. At the same time I am well aware that things are not all that simple, and I know that sometimes the high quality of a work of art is not nullified by its base tendency. And a man is not himself destructive because he holds up the mirror to the distraction and desperation of men. We have but to think of Goya. I am also aware that denunciation and the revelation of the baseness of man can be a true and valid expression of our existence; and that, indeed, such a revelation can have a more positive effect than a striving for the mediocre and the avoidance of extremes. It is no easy matter to determine where the limit lies.

At the same time everything should be done to encourage what needs encouragement in the broad sphere which lies between the mediocre on the one hand and the tendency to destructiveness on the other. I am aware that it requires a certain daring to say this when at the same time I must admit that existing conditions are not favourable, and that we lack the means for this task.

In considering our cultural mission abroad we must not restrict ourselves to the ancient, traditional and hallowed treasures of the German people. Not long ago I read a newspaper report of a German cultural week which described it as 'worthy enough but a bit moth-eaten', and when I looked into the matter I discovered that the reproach was not altogether unjustified. We must try to show that we are not merely living on the cultural heritage of the past. Just now I said a word or two in favour of the moral sciences, and now, appealing quite deliberately to my own experience, I would like to do the same for the natural sciences. Our doctors, our physicists and our research workers have a tremendous task, particularly as they are perhaps ahead of some of their colleagues abroad – I have been told so by German scientists, because perhaps more than others they have overcome pure positivism. In some countries interest in the conclusions of moral science has been replaced by interest in our natural sciences. We must take this into account where lecture series and cultural weeks are concerned. We should consider whether now and again we should not supplement the ponderous, inflexible and objective qualities which are regarded as characteristic of us by something more agreeable and airy, even in the knowledge that this might not have such a lasting effect, but might perhaps be more readily and widely appreciated.

# 16

# Germany and the Political Unification of Europe*

You are gathered here in Wiesbaden to discuss one of the most important questions of our time, the political unification of Europe, and I regard it as a great honour that you should have invited me to address you on the subject, particularly as it is one which has occupied me for a long time now.

Amongst you are many who have worked for years for the political unification of Europe, and some of you have devoted your whole lives to it. There is therefore no need for me to spend any time discussing the reasons which make European political unity a desirable thing. If the voice of Europe is to be heard effectively in the great questions which occupy the world today then the countries of Europe, both the large and the small, must cease to speak with many voices, and determine to come together and pursue a uniform policy. If they fail to do this they will have no opportunity of exercising any permanent influence on the course of events. This is beyond dispute, and so also is the fact that in a tense world situation, which is likely to continue for some time to come, Europe can retain her freedom and her progressive social structure, and safeguard her economic progress, only if she unites. Unity is strength is such a commonplace that one hesitates to say it, but there are so many short-sighted people who would be prepared to sacrifice the great aim of European unity for uncertain or temporary advantages that it must nevertheless be said, and be said very emphatically.

It is true that Europe is protected by her American partner; it is true that this protection will be necessary for a long time to come; and it is true that we must do everything possible to make our

*Speech to the Congress of European Federalists on January 15th 1959.

co-operation with the United States even closer. But this does not alter the fact that in the last resort Europe will survive only if she strengthens herself, and the best way – even the only way – to do this is for her to unite. We can all step up our economic achievements at home, give more assistance to the under-developed countries, and strengthen our defence to the utmost; even so, what we can possibly achieve separately will still lag far behind what we could do together as a European community of States.

It has been said that although all this may be theoretically true it is nevertheless illogical, even illusory, to work for the political unification of Europe, since there is no such thing as a joint European consciousness such as would be necessary to underpin political unification. This strikes me as a very superficial attitude to the problem. In all European countries there is a deeply-rooted belief that the idea of the sovereign State responsible only to itself and fenced off from the outside world must now give way to the idea of a larger community. The consciousness that in striving to maintain the freedom of Europe and safeguard her future we form a real community of interests is more widespread than our critics think.

How can we bring about this political unification we regard as necessary? A great deal has already been done, particularly in the economic field. The European Coal and Steel Community, the Common Market and EURATOM, which embrace six European countries, have already started a development which will ultimately turn six separate economies into one unified one.

The Council of Europe and EURATOM already associate these six countries with eleven others in Europe; and, as you know, negotiations are now in progress for the establishment of a multi-lateral economic association. All concerned are doing their best to overcome the difficulties. If the desired success has not been achieved as soon as we hoped, nevertheless fruitful co-operation between the countries of the Common Market and the other countries of Europe holds great promise for them all, so that all are keenly interested in success. Recognition of this fact justifies our confidence that the negotiations will ultimately prove successful.

Thus although we can say that as far as the economic aspect is concerned the picture is favourable and justifies hope in further developments, we cannot say the same with any confidence about the political sphere, though even here we have succeeded in establishing institutions whose importance should not be underestimated.

NATO has become an indispensable instrument not only of our joint defence but for the political co-ordination of the member States of the Atlantic Community.

The Council of Europe, and in particular its consultative assembly, which is the oldest European parliamentary institution, has discussed a great number of projects which have influenced further developments, in one or two cases decisively. This is all very obvious, but it does not add up to a real political community, because the member States retain the right to differ from their partners in all political questions. One can talk of a political community only if there is a guarantee of united action – at least in all vital questions. It is more difficult to arrive at this in political than in economic matters, but at least we can say with some satisfaction that a start has been made.

The institutions of the three European Communities are the parliament of Europe, the Commission of the European Economic Community, the High Authority, and the Commission of EURATOM. They deal primarily with economic matters, which, however, to some extent directly affect politics, so that in a sense we already have a European political community. Consider, for example, the agreement arrived at recently between EURATOM and the United States Government, which means valuable assistance for the development of nuclear power for peaceful purposes in Europe. Then there is the joint trading policy within the Common Market, which means that the six countries concerned appear increasingly as one at international economic conferences and are represented by joint delegates. How can one fail to see the political significance of these happenings? At the same time these European institutions encourage the growth of confidence between the partners, and this is the essential condition for joint political action.

Here the parliament of Europe is particularly important because as its deputies become convinced that the policy of economic co-operation must ultimately find its apotheosis in political unification, so preparatory steps towards it will be taken.

A great deal has been said and written about the integrating effect of joint parliamentary institutions, and, in fact, politically like-minded deputies have come together irrespective of their various nationalities. Their European responsibilities take precedence over their nationality.

Finally I should like to say a word or two about the immanent logic of these developments: at the end of the transitional period laid down for the Common Market there will be one uniform economy instead of six more or less isolated economies, and then political unification will be inevitable. No unified economy could exist if it were split by political differences; in the long run, therefore, it must lead either to dissolution or political unity.

The chain reaction started by the establishment of the European Coal and Steel Community in 1951 is still proceeding. At the time we said that it was merely a beginning and that the countries concerned would move steadily closer to each other, or the experiment would be a failure. Since then the Common Market and EURATOM have arisen, and it is clearer than ever that economic community must be followed by political community, otherwise we shall find it difficult to maintain our economic gains.

It would be going too far for me to discuss the forms such a political community might take, and I therefore propose to restrict myself to one or two more general observations. When we talk of a European political community the question of its relationship with other European countries immediately arises. As far as the member countries are concerned I should like to make it very clear that just as the European economic communities we have created are not intended to be restrictive, nor would a European political Community be. It would be open to any European country prepared to accept the necessary political conditions in the interests of all. In addition such a political community would maintain the closest possible relationship with the European States outside it, and with other partners throughout the world, either through the already existing European institutions and NATO, or through additional channels.

As our aim is to strengthen Europe and thus the free world as a whole, it is important that our unification should develop organically out of the already existing relationships. This is true in particular of our relationship with Britain, which I certainly realize has thrown in her lot with Europe more than ever before in her history, and shouldered far-reaching responsibilities towards the Continent. It is the main aim not only of British policy, but also that of the Federal Republic and of all other European countries allied with Britain, to maintain and consolidate this relationship in the interests of all. We feel sure that ways and means can be found to do this both economically and politically whether Britain joins the European political community or finds herself unable to take such a far-reaching step.

Another question is the relationship of our common interests to the particular interests of the membership countries. By definition a community presupposes a certain subordination of the individual to the whole. Those who wish to enjoy the advantages of belonging to a larger unity must not study their own interests to an extent which damages the interests of the community as a whole. Now the political situation in Europe today is such that the rightly understood interests of each European State are largely in conformity with the interests of them all.

We Germans have repeatedly had cause to realize this in recent years when we turned to our European partners for support in our efforts to restore the unity of our own country. It was given to us in a proper recognition that the continued dismemberment of Germany damages not only her interests but those of all other European countries; and I acknowledge with particular gratitude the unanimity with which both our European and our American and Canadian partners have demanded guarantees for the freedom of Berlin.

However, we must not overlook the fact that there are other questions in which the same unanimity does not exist, and here we must work for a sensible compromise; either by the gradual subordination of national interests to the interests of the community, or by recognizing, either temporarily or indefinitely, that in certain respects national freedom of action must be allowed to continue.

From what I have said you will have seen that I am convinced that we are well on the way to a European Community. The form in which it ultimately comes about will be determined by the special needs of the member States and because it must be established in close relationship with the other States of Europe and the free world. We may well be encouraged by historical precedents, but we shall have to resolve the problem in new ways arising out of the given situation. The sooner we get down to this task the better it will be for all of us. If your congress helps to persuade people of this then it will have done well.

Do not be disappointed because I have not been content merely to praise the aim, but have also pointed to the difficulties and problems which hedge it about. Deep feeling can perhaps produce more rousing words, but those of us who have to face the facts of everyday life must guard against too much enthusiasm. This does not prevent my saying that we should all be passionately convinced that the path we have taken is right; that it is, indeed, the only way of survival for the continent in which we live and to which we feel ourselves inalienably attached by our history, our tradition and our civilization in a historic world clash we must face whether we like it or not. We have already gone farther along that path than many of our critics have realized. Let us not be influenced in our decisions by them but by the will of our own peoples, and then we shall be well on the way to success.

# 17

# From National States to a United Europe*

I WARMLY welcome the opportunity to address you on the tasks and aims of Germany's European policy. It is not difficult to establish a connection between the political, historical and cultural ideas the word 'Rome' arouses in us and the wishes and hopes of the European peoples today.

The occasion which has brought me – I think I may say – 'back' to Rome, is of great importance not only for European policy in particular, but also for the relations of our two countries. The head of the Italian Government and the German Federal Chancellor are now engaged in a discussion of world political and European questions in a spirit of mutual confidence possible only as between old friends. What brings our Governments and our peoples together again and again is our joint anxiety for the maintenance of that heritage we associate with the word 'Rome', a civilization based on Christian belief and informed by justice and freedom. In the many hundreds of years of our history it has taken on various forms, but in its substance and in its attitude to the rest of humanity it has remained inviolable and unchanged.

Some of you might possibly feel that there are more important and more urgent problems for a German Foreign Minister than European politics. It is quite true that we have suffered set-backs, and that the European peoples who are just recovering from the wounds of war are now menaced with new and serious dangers and find their inner reconstruction hampered and delayed. Could I possibly forget, for example, that the German people are dis-

*Speech delivered on January 23rd 1960 in connection with the official visit of Chancellor Doctor Adenauer to Rome.

membered? And we all know that not only the German people but the whole of humanity longs for peace, freedom and justice.

The statesmen from the East and the West have begun to visit each other's countries again. The heads of Western Governments were in Paris recently to prepare for the so-called East-West Summit, and millions of people on both sides of the Iron Curtain are torn between hopes and fears, wondering whether there really will be a *détente*, or whether what seems to be opening up will be nothing but a new phase of the Cold War.

We all feel that the decision over peace or war is now coming to a head, and this is terrifying in view of the enormously increased means of destruction of our time. Because this is so I want to talk to you today about the ideas of the Federal Government and of the majority of the German people where Europe is concerned. I want to tell you how they see their tasks in relation to their European aims, and how they think they can best and most rapidly be achieved.

I am firmly convinced that the solution to the terrible problems which face us today can best be found in a free, democratic and irrevocable unification of the European peoples. If this old Europe of ours, which was and still is the cradle of human culture, can show a divided world how national conflicts can be peaceably settled, and how the will of its many millions can be united in a desire to create a better and more just world, then I am sure that such an example would work on in the world and awaken new energies. The world in which we live today requires such great human aims.

Our impressive technological progress has not yet succeeded in bringing mankind a little more happiness, a little more security. Fear still dominates the world. But if we succeed in replacing the old national rivalries by jointly held ideals – and this is the true significance of European policy – we shall fill the hearts of our contemporaries with new hope.

Many of us remember the first post-war years and the numerous conferences of those who had pledged themselves to the European cause. In the meantime we have become a little older and more cautious, but we can see that the spontaneous growth of the European idea after the Second World War came about quite simply because human nature was unwilling to accept ruin and destruction as inevitable. In this sense the first stirrings of the European spirit in the years after the war were truly elemental.

This was particularly true of the German people. After years of fatal error they once again had an opportunity of placing their energy and ability behind a policy which represented the best in their political traditions. Parallel with this dawning of a European task the political ideas of the German people also began to turn to federalism. Federalism was understood as a hierarchic structure of communities, each of which was expected to perform those tasks which naturally fell to its lot, and to surrender those tasks beyond its resources to the next higher stage in the hierarchy.

In developing such ideas the German people were able to look back on a rich tradition of federalist thought. The alternatives, Centralism or Federalism, played a big role in the nineteenth century before the founding of the German Reich. Because of this Germans often fail to understand why other peoples, who are familiar only with centralism, find it so difficult to broach the question of renouncing national sovereignty in favour of a federal European State.

Thus when the German people took up the idea of a united Europe after the war, the process did not involve any new and unfamiliar form of political thought for them, and their main object was to learn from the errors of the past.

The fact that from 1952 onwards a practical basis for building up a European community developed increasingly only shows how sound and realistic the assumptions of such a policy really were. Perhaps when the European Coal and Steel Community was first founded it looked no more than a device for resolving Franco-German tension. Nevertheless, and it is indisputable now, it represented an attempt to transfer problems born of a clash of national interests to a higher plane for their solution, and this was the important thing about it.

No one expected this first European community to be the ideal pattern for European co-operation. Economic and political communities of such far-reaching importance cannot receive their final form round a conference table. The very magnitude of the problems involved means that there will have to be corrections here and there in practice. It is not surprising, therefore, that the inner structure of the European nuclear agency and of the Common Market differ from that of the Coal and Steel Community. No one can yet say what the ideal pattern of European co-operation will be. It is a question that only practical experience can settle.

However, the form the co-operation takes is not the important thing. Much more important is the goodwill of those who have decided to go along together, and the weight of the economic, social and political problems to be solved. It would therefore be a mistake to regard the discussion on the form of co-operation as evidence that enthusiasm for a European solution is waning. It is not the means but the end which matters, and geographical and economic conditions still categorically demand European unity. It is up to us to recognize and perform the task history has set our generation.

I am therefore not greatly disturbed because of late European co-operation has experienced a slight shift of accent in the sense that national interests are rather more stressed than before. It is quite natural that each country of the European community should be anxious to ensure that its own fundamental national interest is considered, and it is quite certain that European unity would be an illusion if any attempt were made to establish it at the expense of justifiable national interests. Equally certain, however, is that the joint exercise of our political, economic and military resources will allow a rationalization to the benefit of all.

There has been some dispute as to whether European unity will mean that the former national States will lose their character and personality. Nothing of the sort has happened or will happen. The alternatives 'German or European', 'French or European', just do not exist. The inevitable result of European unity will be that national characteristics – which have, after all, taken hundreds of years to develop – will be enhanced and strengthened by close contact with other nationalities. Multiplicity in unity is our aim.

There has also been some question as to whether the improvement of bilateral relations between European countries should come before multilateral co-operation. The academic question has arisen as to whether good bilateral relations are the preliminary for a European policy, or whether the latter will first bring the peoples of Europe together. We should not allow such theoretical considerations to obstruct our perspective. Once more it has been shown that practical developments are more important than human speculations. Here too there are no fixed alternatives: multilateral and bilateral co-operation supplement each other.

Nothing is better calculated to make the mutual relationship clear than what has happened between France and Germany. Again and again political conflicts between the two peoples have led to disaster not only for them both, but for Europe and the world at large. The

167

most important political task after the Second World War was, therefore, to resolve the Franco-German conflict, and no one need regard the result of these efforts with misgiving.

Whoever desires Franco-German co-operation and true friendship between the two countries based on mutual confidence and a recognition of their joint interests and tasks is certainly not working against the idea of European integration but helping to create its most important condition. European integration is unthinkable as long as there is conflict between France and Germany, whether based on mistrust, fear, resentment, or on economic and political tension. To help us throw off this burden of the past we need a feeling of European solidarity, and understanding co-operation between the European partners. And, in fact, such joint efforts have already brought us along a good stretch of the way.

The relations between Italy and the Federal Republic have always been friendly, and we can see that within the framework of European co-operation they have now become even closer. The discussions taking place here offer a new example of European co-operation entirely different from the classic diplomacy of the eighteenth and nineteenth centuries.

I need hardly say that we are all well aware of the difficulties of such a reorientation of European policy. The establishment of the Common Market influences bilateral relations between the member States and with the countries outside it. As a result there have been changes in competitive conditions on the international market. We are quite conscious of these developments and we have no intention of evading the issues they involve.

We feel that the best way to deal with such difficulties is by stages. Since the Common Market agreement came into force a number of measures have not only increased trade between the members, but also between them and those European countries which are not members, and other, non-European, countries as well, and we propose to continue along these lines. We feel quite sure that the European trade war prophesied by some will not take place, and the Federal Government and its partners are confident that they will be in a position to take whatever measures may be necessary to prevent it.

This was the aim of the conference that took place in Paris a few days ago at the instance of the four heads of government. It demonstrated the firm determination of all the parties concerned to settle those economic differences which have arisen. Personally I have no doubt that their efforts will be successful, and the Federal Government is certainly determined to do everything it can to assist.

I do not propose to deal with the possible solutions now. Not so long ago it was thought that it would be possible to create a larger free-trade area by multilateral agreement, but in my view the discussions within the Common Market have shown that this method is not appropriate, and we must not adopt measures which would create a wider framework whilst destroying the narrower. We must keep the Common Market in order to attain the political objective we set ourselves in the Rome agreements. Beyond this the initiative of the United States and Canada has shown that these countries must not be excluded from the economic developments we are aiming at. I feel, therefore, that we shall succeed only if we guide our actions on the basis of certain principles.

First of all, whatever we do we must make quite certain that the established community of the six European countries does not suffer. This is because it is not only the Common Market we want, even though it does represent an economic community of six countries with a total population of almost 179 million people, but the further development of these countries into a political community, so that Europe's strength and influence in the historic confrontation between East and West may be increased. At the same time we do not want this development to take place at the expense of our friendly relationship with other European countries, and we feel ourselves associated with them and under an obligation to them. I am thinking not only of those countries which belong to the European Free Trade Area, but also of those which belong to neither association.

None of us in the Common Market has the slightest wish to establish any new form of economic autarky. Inter-State traditional relations, whether bilateral or multilateral, are vital to us all, and we should do our best to encourage and extend them. To allow them to decline would not only be economic error but political insanity.

This is no less true of our relations with the United States and Canada, countries with which we are associated in the Atlantic Community. We all realize that it is only in common that we can fulfil the obligations this community imposes on us. Having undertaken them we must co-ordinate our economic interests. The stronger each separate member is the stronger the community will be.

We must therefore consolidate our progress towards European

unity and reject all false and doctrinaire ideas. It would be foolish for us to squabble about ways and means when we are in agreement about aims. At the same time we must guard against any tendency to perfectionism, and in breaking new ground we should remember that the better is only too often the enemy of the good. Should any one of us feel impatient then he need only look back at what we have already accomplished, and remind himself that it is no easy matter to change historically-rooted forms – even when we are all agreed that they need changing. It is very difficult for people to give up ideas into which they were born. However, the State is nothing but a community of people, and people can get used to new ways and be brought to realize that they are better than the old.

I am sure we are all agreed that the dynamic, and even occasionally alarming, developments in world political conditions must be taken into account. It would be dangerous to allow our thinking to become static. In recent years we have seen the development of a new structural order in the world. We may well deplore it, but we cannot change it. We must therefore adapt ourselves to it. Economic areas have extended enormously, and great political changes have taken place within them, raising new problems and facing us with new issues.

Not so long ago Russia was a European country much like others; big certainly, and with a large population and rich material resources, but not outside the category of many other European countries. In the past forty years, however, the communist revolution has changed the face of Russia. One of the most unfortunate results of the last world war was to turn Communism into a dominant force that now influences developments throughout the world. Numerous European States have been incorporated unwillingly into its power orbit.

We Germans have particular cause to appreciate the tragedy and the dangers of this development, because Communism has extended its boundaries right into the heart of our country, and thus into the heart of Europe. Almost eighteen million Germans, together with millions of people in the countries of Eastern Europe, now live unwillingly under the despotism of a system which is utterly foreign to them. And on the other side of Europe Communism has extended its power to the Pacific. All over the world we now have to reckon with its influence, and to remember always that it will stick at nothing to achieve its world revolutionary ends.

One of the instruments it uses is economic expansion, coupled with subversion in other countries, and always in the background the threat of force. In the vast territories under its control the Soviet Union disposes not only of tremendous economic strength, but also of an unprecedented quantity of armaments. The events of recent years have shown us very clearly that the Soviet Union will never hesitate to use this vast strength wherever it has reason to believe that it is unlikely to meet with determined resistance.

No single European country is in a position to meet such a threat with its own resources alone, and we now all realize that only unceasing joint efforts will allow us to survive. The supreme aim of all our efforts must, of course, be to preserve peace. The development of arms techniques in recent years has been so alarming that all those in a position of responsibility know that war in such circumstances might well mean the end of humanity altogether. But to want peace is not enough; we must also work with equal determination for the cause of freedom, since the loss of freedom is perhaps the most terrible result of a world without peace.

I think that we in Europe in particular are entitled to claim with pride that in recent years we have made a decisive contribution to the cause of world peace. National rivalries and conflicts which have threatened the peace of the world for centuries have now been resolved by our joint political efforts. Instead of rivalry there is now a feeling of solidarity, instead of enmity there is now friendship. Our policy of European unity therefore deserves the appreciation and support of all those everywhere who really desire peace.

At the same time we are well aware of our limitations, and none of us has any intention of chasing after a phantom like the idea of turning Europe into a so-called Third Power. Such an idea would represent a foolish over-estimate of our own strength, and it would be dangerous, for it would indicate that we had lost our sense of world political realities. The world political clash in which we are all involved, whether we like it or not, is conducted on one hand by those who uphold freedom, justice and human dignity, and are determined to stand together, against those who, on the other hand, deny these moral values and are prepared to destroy them wherever their efforts to do so do not meet with resolute opposition.

Let us not be deceived by the catchword of co-existence. Only those who are prepared to recognize the integral existence of all others are entitled to talk of co-existence. A system which denies self-determination to millions of people and forces them to live under conditions which are loathsome to them, which does not hesitate to interfere in the internal affairs of other States in order to undermine them, and which constantly preaches world revolution, has no right to talk of co-existence, since it demands for itself what it refuses to others.

For this reason too we cannot aim at becoming a Third Power, but must continue to stand on the side of all those who pledge themselves to freedom and justice. The tangible expression of this solidarity is the Atlantic Community which we have joined as equal partners to carry out our share in a task which none of us can evade.

In so doing we have also undertaken a particular obligation whose fulfilment will further the negotiations which began last week in Paris. I refer to that dangerous gap which has opened up between the economically more highly developed countries and the under-developed countries. The contrast between rich and poor, which has so often bedevilled man's history, now faces us once more in truly global dimensions. We must realize that it may well determine world-political developments in the years to come, and we must do everything in our power to close the gap.

The tremendous technological and economic progress which has taken place in great parts of the world would allow us to resolve this problem if we all worked together for the same aim. But we know that the Soviet Union has different ideas. Soviet economic aid to the under-developed countries is part and parcel of foreign politics; its aim is not to help these countries to a free and independent development, but to bring them under Soviet influence. For this reason our efforts to resolve this great task in our own way must be co-ordinated, since in addition to assisting these countries economically it must be our aim to awaken them to a love of freedom so that in order to keep their own freedom they will place themselves on our side.

Decisive negotiations are ahead. The disarmament committee of the United Nations is about to meet, and a few weeks later the heads of government in the United States, Britain, France and the Soviet Union will meet in Paris.* We all realize that it will be no easy matter to resolve the existing political conflicts, and no one will expect speedy results.

I am confident that those who represent the free world will be fully conscious of their responsibilities, but they will be able to live up to

*The reference is to the unsuccessful Paris Summit Conference in May 1960.

them only if they act together in complete solidarity. The feeling of joint responsibility must unite those who live in freedom with those who have lost it or see it threatened. As a German I am thinking primarily of the millions of my fellow countrymen who have been deprived of their freedom, and of those two and a half million Germans in Berlin who see their freedom threatened, but I am not forgetting those other peoples who have also lost their freedom, but who have given us heroic evidence during the past few years of their profound attachment to freedom.

The European States cannot do better than continue along the path they have already chosen, and I am convinced that the resurgence of European consciousness will persuade others to go along too. It is our duty so to act that those who do not yet fully realize the value of such solidarity may become convinced.

# 18

# On the Future of the Atlantic Community*

ONLY a few days ago your new President frankly expressed his anxiety about the present state of the Western system of alliances, and in particular NATO.

We and our other allies in Europe are moved by the same anxiety. Let us therefore discuss the situation frankly, find out where the fault lies, and decide what can be done to remedy matters. We must not hesitate to criticize even if it is painful, and we must not evade any calls even if they are on ourselves. Before this audience there is no need for me to describe the origin and development of NATO, but I will recall that up to the foundation of NATO the Soviet Union had forced over a hundred million people in Europe under communist domination, and added something like 600,000 square miles of territory to its empire. Its last attempt to continue its expansionist policy in Europe began with the blockade of Berlin, which ended at about the same time that NATO was founded. If I mention the renewed threat to Berlin it is not in order to bring up the many-sided German question for discussion. But I do feel that the attitude of the Soviet Union to Berlin now and in the immediate future can be taken as a gauge of its judgement of the degree of solidarity and resistance of the Western world.

There is no doubt that during the past twelve years the economic strength and the military might of the Soviet Union have steadily increased. In 1949 Soviet atomic armaments were only just beginning, whilst those of the United States were already highly developed. Today there are various indications that in some respects the Soviet

*Address to the Council on Foreign Relations on February 15th 1961 during a visit to the United States when Doctor von Brentano met President Kennedy.

Union has caught up with the United States in atomic armaments and rockets. This is also true of numerous other aspects of armaments – for example, the Red submarine fleet. Parallel to this increase in military strength there has been quite considerable economic development, and this has been enhanced by co-ordination with the economies of the satellite States. This progress has increased Soviet confidence and led to political activity and expansionism all over the world. So far it is not clear whether the rise of Chinese Communism will reinforce Soviet power or be to its disadvantage. It may well be that there is serious tension between the two communist powers, probably based on profound ideological disputes. Such conflicts may well affect the attitude of the Soviet Union to the Western world in the future, but I feel that it would be dangerous if we were already to count this situation as a factor favouring Western policies.

The situation in the Western camp is not so clear either. The past twelve years have certainly seen considerable economic progress and healthy recovery, and considerable efforts have been made to strengthen our defence, which has led to a feeling of increased security. Thanks to American assistance free Europe has become stronger so that it now represents a significant part of the potential of the free world. But we must not deceive ourselves; the balance of power between East and West, which we have managed to maintain with such difficulty, can swing against us at any moment. The so-called 'uncommitted' world, the awakening peoples of Asia and Africa, is still hesitant. In their efforts to obtain political independence these peoples are inclined to overlook the very real threat to their freedom in the future.

The free countries of the world tend dangerously to subordinate their security to the improvement of their living standards, unmindful of the fact that social well-being will not be able to survive political and military pressure backed up by superior atomic rockets. This is true not only of security but also of science and technology. The achievements of European and American scientists during the past hundred years have been tremendous, but this would be nothing but an idle memory if technological development in the West were to lag behind the Soviet Union now.

So much for the situation today. What role is NATO playing in it? Has it failed or can it help us to resolve our difficulties?

Let us take a look at the Washington Pact, which represents the constitution of NATO. In its classic brevity and simplicity it leaves

175

no room for ambiguity. Only its first five articles are of decisive importance. Of these only Article 5 concerns the obligation to lend military aid. Articles 1 to 4 embrace far-reaching undertakings which are primarily of a political or economic nature, and if they are known at all to public opinion in general they are certainly regarded as a sort of accompanying political flourish. Even in informed circles, including governments, NATO is often exclusively regarded as a military alliance deriving its particular importance from the magnitude of the threat it is designed to meet, but for the rest is no different from any other military coalition.

But this is an error and perhaps it has been responsible for some of the mistakes and failures of recent years. If we regard the strongest bond in the West as a purely military alliance then we shall be inclined to look at all the problems of the present-day world from the angle, or largely from the angle, of military security. But paradoxically such an attitude represents a very real danger to military preparedness and watchfulness. If the enemy were to alter his tactics and temporarily withdraw the military threat, and begin to operate in an outwardly conciliatory fashion, the military threat would also begin to recede in the consciousness of the peoples of the free world and there would be a consequent tendency to neglect our defence efforts. A tangible sign of this dangerous development is the discussion now taking place concerning a reduction of national defence budgets and a shortening of the period of military service.

On the other hand, a one-sided interpretation of NATO as a military defence coalition involves the danger that the military authorities and their purely military demands would attain a disproportionate influence on policy. With this we touch upon a fundamental principle of the Western world. For us politics can never be a function of politico-military thought, but the responsible organization of all the vital forces of a nation, to which its defence apparatus must definitely be subordinated.

A system of alliances such as NATO, which sets itself far-reaching tasks and objectives in its Preamble and in certain of its Articles, cannot restrict itself to military matters and the passive work of organizing the defence, but must regard its most important task as the creation of a better future. Every measure we take and every decision we come to must tend to serve the cause of peace today and in the future.

Once this background is accepted the tasks the Cold War imposes on us, including military and other deterrent measures, and the ability to wage a hot war if we must, fall logically into place and in their right proportions. Their aim is to safeguard peace and to keep open the path to a better world order.

Despite the great stress placed on the military task of NATO we cannot unfortunately say that its military strength is adequate. The *élan* of the first years, brought about largely by the shock of naked communist aggression in Korea, and culminating in the military decisions of the NATO council in Lisbon in February 1952, has faded. Constant high pressure is disagreeable, and such things as elections and domestic political struggles demand their tribute. All these things are well known to us as accompanying features of the democratic way of life, which, in our view, is the only one which safeguards man's freedom, and is therefore the only lasting form of government. But the price of liberty is eternal vigilance: *Vigilia Pretium Libertatis*, as the motto at the headquarters of the European NATO forces declares. But such vigilance demands a great degree of discipline, and even sacrifices, so the hesitation is understandable. Nevertheless we must demand such discipline and such sacrifices from our peoples, our parliaments and our governments. Just as the individual member of a family must subordinate himself to its interests as a whole, so our countries and their governments must consciously recognize a certain degree of interdependence in the interests of the independence and freedom of all.

The danger of war can be reduced without any threat to our freedom only if we are at least as strong as our potential enemy. This applies not only to the number of divisions and artillery strength, but also every bit as urgently to the brain behind our defence preparations, our political leadership, which is at least as important as the state of our armaments.

We have to face a politically fanatical enemy who wields his military strength ruthlessly under a united and centralized command. We are fifteen free nations with fifteen independent armies. In addition each one of these nations has its own aims and tasks, which also have to be served by its armed forces, so that only part of these forces is at NATO's disposal.

This may be politically understandable and even inevitable, but what is neither is that NATO's armed forces are not under one supreme commander with clearly defined powers. There are four different commands (Europe, the Atlantic, the Channel, and Canada

177

and the United States). Their commanders are not subordinate to one supreme commander, but to a Military Committee, with another body, the Standing Group, for military planning – not for command purposes – above it, below it or beside it. Theoretically all these bodies are subordinate to the political leadership of the NATO Council, which could hardly prove efficient in an emergency, since its permanent members, the NATO ambassadors, are dependent on instructions from their own governments. In peace time the commanders, General Norstad in Europe, for example, have no authority over the forces of the alliance, and only a limited one even in war time. A British battalion could not be moved from north to south Germany. This is not entirely due to lack of command authority, but also to the fact that logistics is a matter for each national command. For example, the weapons, equipment, transport, spare parts, munitions and so on, held in South Germany are suitable for American units, but not for the German, British and French units under the same commander.

The longest distance between the Iron Curtain and the Atlantic is five hundred miles, a distance that can be covered by a modern aircraft within a matter of minutes. Nevertheless, this exiguous space is divided up into various air defence zones under a variety of commands, since national touchiness has so far permitted no other arrangement.

I have mentioned only two examples from a long list of organizational inadequacies, and it is no business of mine to cope with the detailed military problems involved. What interests me is the political problem which arises because our policy of deterrence is not as credible as it might be; and, indeed, cannot be so long as we do not organize our defence effectively.

For this reason we gratefully welcome the proposal made by the United States Government last December for the establishment of a unified NATO nuclear force as part of the long-term planning of the NATO Council.* At last this represents a step towards a unified and centralized NATO command. Final decisions have not yet been taken, and a good many difficult problems must first be resolved, including that of United States legislation, and the strengthening of Europe's voice in the control of our nuclear defence force. But whatever answer

*The United States Secretary of State Christian A. Herter had proposed the formation of a multilateral force equipped with medium-range ballistic missiles as part of NATO.

is ultimately found, under no circumstances must NATO's military strength be compromised.

Let us now turn from theoretical military questions to the very practical sphere of the Cold War in which the historical world struggle between the two opposing camps is being fought, and in which two opposing ideologies are competing for the souls of those in areas not yet committed, and unwilling to commit themselves.

In the military sphere Western man is interested only in defence, but in the Cold War we must act positively. We shall make no progress on the way to a better world order if we entrench ourselves behind a political Maginot line of illusory safety and wait for the attacks of the enemy before we defend ourselves.

We are fighting in a good cause, so why do we constantly seem to be half-ashamed of it? Are our ideas of freedom and justice, peace and well-being not noble and cogent? For two thousand years and more men have suffered and died for them. Have we now even lost the power of communicating our ideals to others? We should not regard political propaganda as beneath our dignity. If the people of some young country fall victim to crude Soviet propaganda not all our wisdom and refinement will prevent them from taking the side of world Communism against us. The danger of this sort of thing is reflected in the voting in international organizations such as the United Nations. So far the members of NATO have not succeeded in agreeing amongst themselves on a uniform line in what, for want of a better expression, is known as psychological warfare. And yet we have the enormous advantage that our propaganda could be based on truth and reality, and not, like communist propaganda, on lies and slander. The founders of the North Atlantic Pact recognized the existence of this task in Article 2 which declares that the member States shall contribute to the development of peaceable and friendly international relations by consolidating their own free institutions and seeking a greater understanding for the principles on which these institutions are based.

One special aspect of our relations with the under-developed countries is involved here It is certainly not NATO's business to organize joint actions in any of them, but it certainly is a most urgent and typical task of the alliance to hold joint discussions concerning any measures calculated to forestall dangerous Soviet activities and assist the peoples of these countries not only to attain their freedom but to safeguard it.

With this we come to the question of political consultation: something of which we all approve in theory, but few carry out satisfactorily in practice. Article 4 provides for consultation between the partners when in the opinion of any one of them the inviolability of its territory, its political independence or its security is menaced. This article is so definite and so comprehensive that all important world political matters could be brought before the NATO Council for discussion. And yet again and again we find that questions of vital importance are either not discussed at all, or that after the discussion the differences between the partners remain irreconcilable. There is no point in fiddling with methods of procedure, such as introducing a formal obligation for consultation. We are faced here with a real dilemma which derives from the fact that in the last resort any country will act according to its own ideas, even though no one else understands them. It will no doubt be influenced by individual and collective decisions, but, even so, these derive from its own vital sphere. As soon as a country feels its own vital interests to be at stake the subjective borderline of loyalty to its allies is reached, and this, of course, is particularly dangerous in the case of NATO, which exists to safeguard us all. Political wisdom demands that we should refrain from formulating or interpreting agreements too harshly. If we do so refrain this borderline may never be reached, or, indeed, drawn at all. None of us should be perfectionists and demand more from our allies than we are ourselves able or prepared to grant.

At the same time, a recognition of this should not prevent us from constantly doing our utmost to improve, broaden and strengthen the process of joint consultation.

An appreciation of the limitations inevitable in our alliance also offers us perhaps some indication of NATO's position in the future peaceful order we are all working for. I am thinking here both of the shape of the free world, that is to say of the inner arrangements of the West, and of the future of the world as a whole.

As far as our own arrangements in the West are concerned we regard NATO as a defensive wall behind which we can settle our own affairs without outside interference. We have not yet found its ultimate form, and perhaps we never shall, but we must tirelessly work for improved solutions. Personally I feel that we can already look back on a sufficient number of successes amply to justify our continuing along the path we have chosen. To illustrate what I mean let me mention developments in the German Federal Republic. In the years following the complete collapse of the Third Reich we have succeeded in establishing a solidly based democratic order. This was possible only because the free world was prepared to accept Germany into the community of free peoples and thus enable the German people to carry out their reconstruction. Today the Federal Republic is an integral part of the free world, and the German people are determined to extend and consolidate this relationship and never live without it again. It is, God knows, not the fault of the Germans that the spirit of intolerance, injustice and the concentration camp still prevails in that part of Germany which is still unfree. The régime there is wholly and solely the responsibility of the Soviet Union.

Then there is the fundamentally new and friendly relationship which now exists between the German and the French peoples after centuries of enmity and conflict, a relationship based on sincerity, good sense and conviction.

Let me also mention the daring idea of a supra-national community through which for the first time an attempt is being made to change and perhaps altogether replace the old idea of the national State by a higher form of political existence embracing many peoples. The Schuman Plan, the Common Market, and EURATOM may not be perfect solutions in themselves, but they form a solid basis on which we can build a political community. I do not regard the differences at present existing between the 'Six' and the 'Seven', which are causing you and us a good deal of anxiety, as an evidence of failure, but rather as a challenge to us to find new ways and means by which we can come closer together. We are firmly convinced that the newly-formed OECD will also serve this purpose. In the last resort all these efforts are only an attempt to find an organizational framework for spiritual, political and economic realities.

The domestic problems of the West require treatment in broader scope than my present subject offers, and I will therefore not deal with them further now. As I have already said, I do not feel that NATO is necessarily part and parcel of our Western arrangements but rather the watchdog whose job it is to see that we can settle them amongst ourselves without outside interference.

But NATO is all the more important as a regulating factor in the efforts of the free peoples to determine the future of our world. The Preamble of the North Atlantic Treaty declares:

'The Parties to this Treaty reaffirm their faith in the purposes and principles of the Charter of the United Nations and their desire to live in peace with all peoples and all Governments.'

'They are determined to safeguard the freedom, common heritage and civilization of their peoples, founded on the principles of democracy, individual liberty and the rule of law.'

'They are resolved to unite their efforts for collective defence and for the preservation of peace and security.'

The starting point is thus an acceptance of the United Nations Organization. The founders of NATO made it perfectly clear that NATO had been established in accordance with the charter of the United Nations and that it would operate exclusively within those limits. Incidentally, the Government of the German Federal Republic takes the same attitude. Against the will of the German people and their government Germany is not a member of the United Nations, but when she joined the North Atlantic Pact she solemnly declared that her policy would be in accordance with the principles of the United Nations and that she would accept the obligation imposed by Article 2.

If a day comes when all peoples make the Charter of the United Nations the basis of their policy then NATO will become unnecessary, but at present the United Nations Organization definitely needs NATO and the balance of power it has created towards that other system which, in the words of President Kennedy, seeks to turn the United Nations into an arena of the Cold War.

The common attitude of the NATO partners to the United Nations is, incidentally, not the same as a common attitude within it. It would be pointless to deny that not only do deep differences exist, but that they often come into the open. And these differences exist not only between the NATO States, but also within them. The attitude to the future of those colonial areas which have won their freedom and independence is a typical example. No one denies the basic right of self-determination and freedom for all peoples, but in everyday politics this right is bound up with the need to safeguard the freedom of these peoples. We should not be living up to our responsibility towards these young nations if we stood by and watched them fall, thanks to a misunderstanding of real freedom, into that utter lack of freedom Communism represents. The fate of the peoples of Central and Eastern Europe shows that in reality Communism represents a particularly evil form of colonialism.

Similar problems arise in connection with our relationship to those European countries which are at the moment under Soviet domination.

In the last resort, therefore, we are brought face to face with the possibilities and limits of political consultation. When all allowance is made for the important factors which govern the political attitude of the member States we still cannot afford disunity. An argument which finds no support in the United Nations is useless. It is better that we should adopt one which, while it may not be quite in accordance with our views, tends in the right direction and has a chance of general acceptance. Sometimes I have the feeling that Western States are harsher in their attitude to their allies than to their enemies. It would surely be better for us to show a united front towards the enemy even if it is arrived at by accepting compromises with our friends.

Whether it is a question of future summit conferences, or other East-West discussions about disarmament, or United Nations problems, the West must show a greater realization of the dangers of disunity than it has done in the past. Each partner must refrain from insisting rigidly on his particular standpoint when to do so might threaten the unity of the free world. At the very least we must all of us be prepared to listen sympathetically to the arguments of our friends – we have to listen to the arguments of our enemies whether we like it or not. In particular this means that we should not hesitate to raise the question of joint consultation in NATO even when we know the proposal will meet with resistance.

While acknowledging the democratic principle of equal rights for all members of our international organizations we must not fail to realize that the Soviet Union recognizes only one power as on a par with itself – the United States. This circumstance imposes a special responsibility on the United States, and at the same time gives it a claim to a special position amongst its allies. There is hardly one of us who does not recognize this, and it gives the United States the right to demand the same sacrifices and efforts from its allies as it is prepared to make itself. NATO is not a club for the defence of Europe by the United States, but a necessary association based on mutual assistance. Throughout the years we have been given impressive proofs of American aid and solidarity: the Marshall Plan, the agreement to keep United States troops stationed in Europe, and, recently, the agreement to maintain United States nuclear weapons on the continent for the duration of the NATO treaty.

In April 1949 the former American Secretary of State, Dean Acheson, gave a clear definition of the term 'mutual assistance', and the other partners might well adopt it:

'Article 3 (of the North Atlantic Treaty) does not bind the United States to the proposed military assistance programme, nor indeed to any programme. It does bind the United States to the principle of self-help and mutual aid. Within this principle, each Party to the Pact must exercise its own honest judgement as to what it can and should do to develop and maintain its own capacity to resist and to help others.'

In this spirit the Federal Government has, during the past few months, examined what it can do to help resolve the United States balance of payments difficulties.

In 1955, when I also had the honour of addressing you, I pointed out that 'the Soviet version of relaxing tension has the advantage of being very attractive to all easy-going – I even venture to say cowardly—tendencies. . . . But I believe that if the free world were foolish enough to fall in with Russian plans we should soon find ourselves in a process of dissolution, and to maintain its vital interests the free world would then have to make a very much greater effort than is necessary now'.

I am afraid the situation today is less favourable than it was then, and we are all to some extent responsible. Each of us must now make a great effort, and we look to you to lead the way – not as a shield behind which we can go on living comfortably, but as the leader of a community of free peoples who are anxious to safeguard a worthwhile life in peace and freedom for future generations.

Allow me to summarize these few remarks:

1. NATO was founded in answer to a tangible political and military threat which crystallized in the happenings in Prague and the blockade of Berlin. Perhaps it was then that the free world first clearly recognized what had already happened in Poland, Roumania, Bulgaria and Hungary;

2. The political and military threat to the free world has not diminished in the meantime. The interpretation Moscow places on the idea of co-existence is evidence enough that the Soviet Union

has not abandoned its world-revolutionary aims. On the contrary, compared with 1949 the danger has increased; and so too has the military strength of the Soviet Union. Since then other areas of conflict have been added to that in Europe – Korea, Laos and Tibet in Asia, the Congo in Africa, and Cuba in Central and South America, to mention but a few;

3. In the meantime, too, NATO has justified its existence. It has called a halt to the advance of Communism, at least in Europe. Communism has made no further progress in those territories under NATO protection;

4. NATO will be able to carry out its tasks only if a balance is maintained in arms technique, and this will require ceaseless and supplementary armament efforts by all the NATO partners;

5. The homogeneity of the Communist Bloc demands a similar homogeneity on the part of NATO even though it is based on the voluntary co-operation of sovereign States. In view of modern technical developments the NATO forces will be able to carry out their defence tasks only if all concerned are ready to agree to the greatest possible degree of integration;

6. Adequate integration presupposes the establishment of a common political will. Military power cannot be an end in itself. A unified political leadership is necessary to build it up and use it. The acute observation of a French statesman during the defence community discussions also applies to NATO: 'There have perhaps been countries without an army, but there has probably never been an army without a country';

7. If we must reorganize the command authority in NATO in order to achieve the greatest possible degree of integration, then at the same time we must strengthen our political co-operation. This is all the more necessary because of the interdependence of political problems throughout the world. What happens in Africa or Asia directly concerns those countries primarily affected, for example the member States of SEATO, but indirectly it concerns all members of NATO, since anything involving a member State, such as the military involvement of Holland in Indonesia, weakens NATO as a whole. A united political attitude should be forged in joint consultation;

8. This is particularly true of the United States, which has undertaken world-wide obligations. We must all draw our own conclusions from the frank acknowledgement of the American Secretary of State,

185

Dean Rusk, that the power of the United States has limited its sovereignty. He points out with truth that any decisions made must take into account the needs and hopes of all those who have thrown in their lot with the United States. But this requires that all members of the alliance should adopt the same attitude towards the United States;

9. The logical conclusion from all this is that the United States has the right, and, indeed, the obligation, as the strongest power in the free world and the strongest link in our defence chain, to take over the tasks of leadership even more definitely than before;

10. The obligation which devolves upon the other members of the alliance is to do nothing which might weaken NATO. For example, our united Europe policy must lead to a strengthening of the West, and it is in this spirit and with this objective that the Six have come together. They have no intention of developing any defence conception of their own. Defence is a task which must be carried out inside NATO. The growing economic strength and political importance of their association is at the service of NATO. However, the tension between the Common Market of the Six and the Free Trade Area of the Seven is a serious embarrassment. One of the tasks of OEDC will be to resolve this tension, and here, too, the United States will bear special leadership responsibilities;

11. Aid to the under-developed countries is not a specific NATO task. On the other hand, the free world is engaged in a conflict with Communism in these countries, and therefore this activity must also be seen from a foreign-political standpoint and co-ordinated appropriately. The OECD should therefore undertake or occasion such measures bilaterally or multilaterally in our joint interests;

12. Amongst NATO's tasks will be the preparation of disarmament negotiations, or, more properly, all the negotiations concerning an effective control of armaments. Even if these negotiations take place in a different framework, say, as previously within the United Nations, NATO must still take part in the preparations;

13. The need for this co-operation applies not only to the question of the control of armaments, and the work of political co-ordination within NATO should if possible be extended to include co-operation with other alliances, for example, SEATO. What I have in mind here is the presence of the Secretaries-General of these two organizations at the sessions of the Council of Ministers;

14. It also strikes me that political co-ordination should also

extend to questions which are discussed and decided in the United Nations Assembly. The allies in NATO should not face each other as opponents there. The attempts of the Soviet Bloc to misuse and disrupt the United Nations must not be allowed to succeed. The United Nations must remain an effective instrument in the hands of the free peoples of the world for the extension and consolidation of their freedom.

I am well aware that in this brief talk, which, incidentally, I had very little time to prepare, I have been able to give only very inadequate replies to the questions put to me. However, if I have understood you correctly, all you wanted me to do was to open the discussion, and I hope that by my critical analysis of the present situation, and by the questions I have raised with regard to the future, I may have achieved this.

# 19

# On the Relation of Foreign and Economic Policies*

VERY strangely, foreign policy and economic policy are often regarded as rival spheres of political activity, and for this reason I particularly welcome your invitation to address you on the relationship between the two. There is no general answer in terms of the precedence of one over the other, or in terms of the supposed disputes between the Foreign Office and the Ministry of Economics concerning questions of jurisdiction.

Unfortunately we frequently meet with this superficial attitude. It may sound more sensational, but it does not touch the real essence of the problem. When our foreign and our economic policies do seem to clash then it is no question of a dispute between Erhard and Brentano, but of a real political problem, the sort of conflict of interests familiar to all German industrialists; and the fact is that they cannot resolve all economic questions from an exclusively economic standpoint either. They too have political responsibilities. Their social and national obligations may require decisions which seem for the time being to clash with their economic interests, although I am sure that in the long run what is politically right will always prove to be economically sound. It is part of the great traditions you represent that Germany's employers should avoid one-sidedness and narrow-mindedness and act in the general interests, that they should be political in the best sense of the term.

I have not come here as Foreign Minister to claim precedence for foreign policy. Theoreticians may hold other views, but those of us who bear the direct political responsibility know that it would be

*Speech delivered on May 17th 1961 on the hundredth anniversary of the founding of the German Industrial and Commercial Congress.

unrealistic to adopt such an uncompromising standpoint. On the other hand, it would be no less unrealistic and dangerous to turn Rathenau's famous phrase 'The economy is our fate' into a generalization and conclude that the economy must take precedence. The truth is that foreign policy and economic policy are inter-dependent. Your report for the year 1960–61 gives us a good example of this. It points out that it will prove possible to bridge the differences between the Common Market and the European Free-Trade Area only if all the countries concerned have the political will to do so.

The preliminary condition for a successful foreign policy is a stable domestic order; and this in its turn is possible only on the basis of sound economic principles and healthy social relations.

But a successful foreign policy does not depend entirely on the situation at home, and we must realize more and more clearly that the relationship between one people and another is greatly influenced by whether the other also enjoys stable economic conditions. Now we are in a position to assist our neighbour in this respect, and it seems important to me that there is a growing understanding for this connection between foreign policy and economic policy.

It would be wrong, and even dangerous, if we were to allow our foreign policy to become dependent on our economic policy. On the other hand, we should be abandoning the principle of freedom, which we uphold in the economic sphere also, if we allowed our economic policy to become a mere appendage of our foreign policy. The political responsibility we bear towards our own people is indivisible, and our responsibilities towards other peoples are embraced by it. Thus our task is to find a synthesis between these two spheres, which do not exclude but mutually condition each other.

There is a growing recognition of this nowadays. After the Second World War the bitter lessons of the past helped to bring about a new political attitude – sometimes referred to rather slightingly as 'the conference craze'. But let me tell you from my own practical experience that it has helped us to achieve a degree of international co-operation very much greater than anything that went before. Despite occasional critical moments, the method has saved us from any very serious political and economic set-backs.

Outside Germany there was, even during the war, a growing realization that world economic chaos, the dissolution of traditional world economic relations, and the disintegration of the currency system and of world trade, had also contributed greatly to the catastrophe in human affairs. Following on an attempt to achieve political objectives with unsuitable and therefore ineffective economic means, the thirties saw new errors piled on old. Each country sought to resolve its own problems with its own resources and in its own way. The result was increasing isolation – primarily economic in the first place. Trade and payment barriers, currency and import restrictions cut peoples off from each other. Efforts to establish autarky, together with a strictly bilateral trade policy, sent world trade into a progressive decline; and this was accompanied by a currency chaos that strikes us today as utterly irresponsible. Most currencies suffered violent oscillations and depreciations whose extent was an alarming reflection of the general lack of confidence and economic responsibility that prevailed. All hope of ever returning to stable relationships seemed lost for good. In those unfortunate years each country saw only its own economic difficulties and its own anxieties. And just as the world was caught up in petty economic egoism, so in the political sphere it was the victim of a narrow-minded nationalism that made it selfish and suspicious. Foreign policy and economic policy certainly supplemented and mutually influenced each other then, but in the worst possible way.

Nowadays, in the Western world at least, leading statesmen realize that politico-economic errors can have fateful foreign-political consequences, and that a foreign policy dictated by nationalistic selfishness cuts the ground from under economic well-being and healthy progress. Even whilst the Second World War was still going on a new kind of international co-operation began both economically and politically, and very soon after the war the German people were given an opportunity to learn that economic co-operation can prepare the way for political understanding. The United Nations added to its World Security Council, its leading political body, a corresponding economic body, the Economic and Social Council. In the spirit of international co-operation upheld by the Western world there then followed the Bretton Woods Agreement, which brought back order to our international currency arrangements. The International Currency Fund and the World Bank were established, both of which now seem ideally constituted to play a leading role in the resolution of two of our most urgent world problems: the maintenance of currency stability in the Western world and aid for the under-developed countries. The efforts to restore order to our international currency were soon followed by the Magna Carta of world trade, the General Agreement on Tariffs and Trade, known as GATT. All these institutions are something more than mere instruments designed to deal with limited economic and currency problems; they represent an expression of the determination of all the countries concerned to arrive at a sensible and peaceable way of living together.

In this connection we must not fail to mention the truly great action in which foreign policy and economic policy combined after the Second World War – the Marshall Plan, that great American constructive work on behalf of Europe, which had its origin not in economic considerations, but was the result of a deliberate, courageous and far-sighted foreign policy decision designed to bring the whole of Europe back to political peace and stability by means of economic reconstruction. Unfortunately, owing to the bitter opposition of the Soviet Union, which went so far as the overthrow of the Government in Czechoslovakia, this great American plan could be carried out in part of Europe only. Today we can say that this free part of Europe no longer represents a desperate political problem despite the terrible blows it had to suffer.

Here economic policy worked as a mediator and harbinger of political co-operation. Whether you have the European Common Market in mind or – with well-founded hope – an even larger European community, one thing is clear: common sense in economics coupled with a political aim offers the free peoples of Europe the prospect of a happier future. Recent European developments graphically illustrate the interdependence of foreign and economic policy: the economic community of the six European States in the Common Market cannot be an end in itself. To dismantle the customs barriers in at least part of Europe and create a larger and homogeneous economic area is certainly a big and sensible objective, but the structural character we have given to the European Coal and Steel Community and, in a different way, to the Common Market, demonstrates that we want something more than a multilateral agreement which can be ended by any of the partners. Our economic co-operation is intended to lead to a political community; and anyone who recognizes the interdependence of economic and foreign policy decisions will regard this as logical and natural.

Recent developments have also persuaded Britain to reconsider her position. We appreciate the particular difficulties caused for her in this respect by the continued existence of the Commonwealth, but it strikes me as very favourable that Britain should be prepared to make serious efforts to take part in the economic and political integration of Europe. This development is cogent proof that economic decisions can have political consequences, which, in their turn, lead to far-reaching foreign policy developments.

But there are limits to the concordance of foreign policy and economic policy, and we should have reached an ideal state of affairs if we could say that what we regard as economically good we can also always regard as good from the point of view of foreign policy, and vice-versa. Ideals seldom become realities, and this is particularly true of politics, of course. As statesmen we have to keep our eye on realities and recognize the limits of our possibilities.

As soon as we have to do with systems in which our own ideas of freedom and human dignity no longer apply, and which adopt political methods of which we do not approve but which we have to reckon with, the relationship between foreign and economic policy changes completely. For the Soviet Bloc economics is an instrument of power politics and even revolutionary aims. From our standpoint such an economic policy is not sound and healthy, since it degrades economics to an instrument of demagogic, ideologically-committed power politics. However, I do not think that in the long run it will be possible for the Soviet Bloc to ignore the just claims of its own population for decent living standards, and continue to exploit economics as an instrument of foreign policy. There must come a time when people get tired of propaganda which invents a non-existent danger, or puts forward an unobtainable objective, in order to justify the renunciation of well-being and personal freedom. We can therefore not express too often or too clearly our willingness to co-operate with all peoples in order to bring about social and economic progress all over the world. This offer can be taken up the moment the Soviet Bloc abandons its aggressive policy.

Until it does it will not be possible for us to enjoy the same sort of relationship with it as we do with our Western partners. For compelling political reasons trade and payments have to remain under strict political control in all the countries of the Soviet Bloc. The general rule in dealings with such countries is therefore bilateral agreements, usually involving rather arduous negotiations annually for their extension. Economic interests have often to give way to political necessities, and the precedence of foreign policy is absolute. At least it guards us against economic illusions. Our own security and our political independence must have absolute precedence over economic expediency.

Any economic expediency which undermined fundamental political necessities would be self-deception. For example, it would be politically intolerable for our economy to become dependent in whole or in part on supplies from the Soviet Bloc, or on markets in those countries. I am also quite certain that it would contradict the sound economic interests both of the individual firm and of our economy as a whole to become wholly or largely dependent on markets whose capacities and requirements are subordinate to political considerations. Whoever controls such markets will always be in a position to exploit any temporary economic crisis for foreign political ends.

However, I am not saying anything against normal trading relations with the Soviet Bloc, since we must also bear the possibility of future developments in mind. Nevertheless, we must always remember that the principles of a free economy are not directly applicable to such trading. It is not our fault that we have to make such provisos, but theirs.

Our natural and organic trading relations with the friendly countries of the free world make it relatively easy for us in our direct relations with the Soviet Bloc to cope with the fact that its economic system is quite ruthlessly subordinated to its ambitions in the field of foreign policy. But the situation created by this Soviet policy becomes much more complicated when we are dealing with countries which are anxious to avoid any kind of political dependence on either East or West, and this is particularly true of the under-developed countries. In view of the magnitude of the economic and financial interests involved, aid to these countries is quite clearly properly the business of the State as such, though this does not mean that private initiative on the part of individual firms need be excluded. However, I must also point out that we are necessarily faced here with a task belonging to our foreign policy as such, because the economic strategy of the Soviet Bloc countries, being subordinated to power-politics, has turned the under-developed countries into what is perhaps a decisive political factor in the struggle between the two worlds.

I need hardly stress that here, too, of course, foreign policy does not operate in a vacuum, and that its efforts would be useless without the active and understanding co-operation of economic interests.

Naturally foreign policy must not ignore the reasonable requirements of economic policy. However, it will sometimes be compelled to put political considerations in the foreground even when there are cogent economic arguments on the other side. This is a situation in which foreign policy must take precedence.

Our policy towards the under-developed countries must be the result of a constant weighing of economic and foreign political considerations. With it we have entered a sphere in which we will have to demonstrate that we are capable of establishing harmonious co-operation between foreign policy and economic interests. In my view there is no doubt that we shall be successful provided that we continue as hitherto to approach all problems undogmatically, to weigh up our chances and our interests soberly, to enjoy the support of our economy, and to join in systematic international co-operation to aid the under-developed countries. We shall be working not only for our own interests, but for a new young world, and for the happiness and well-being of all those who want to live in peace and freedom. We shall be working to prevent any recurrence of those political and economic catastrophes from which humanity has suffered in the past.

The programme of your anniversary celebration indicates that the representatives of politics and economics are aware of their joint responsibilities, and are anxious for mutual co-operation. When I was preparing my address to you I looked through your congress report for 1911, that is to say, the fiftieth anniversary of your foundation. It says:

> 'Our congress has no easy task. The authorities are not readily approachable, and there are many royal and ducal officials who feel it beneath their dignity to negotiate with representatives of commerce. Unfortunately employers show very little willingness to take part in politics. And the political parties are not inclined to put forward candidates from amongst us.'

The proceedings at your congress are proof for me that these regrets, and this resignation, no longer exist today. At least I can assure you that there are no such haughty officials in my department. And as far as the political party to which I belong is concerned I can assure you that we greatly value the political co-operation of responsible employers, and that, in fact, we regard it as essential at all levels of our parliamentary democracy. And may I perhaps interpret the invitation you have addressed to me to come here and talk to you as an indication that you are much more inclined to take part in politics than your predecessors were in 1911? If this accurately reflects the feeling of all of us then we can mutually congratulate ourselves on the success of your congress.

# 20

# In Gratitude to Robert Schuman*

I AM truly delighted to be here today in the old Rathaus of the city of Aachen, to congratulate you, President Schuman, on receiving the Karls Prize from the city. At the same time I need not stress how much the Reich's Chancellor regrets not being here to express his good wishes in person.

I am also happy to greet the other recipients of the Karls Prize who are here today, Count Coudenhove-Kalergi, President Monnet and Professor Brugmanns; and those who are not present: Sir Winston Churchill, President Spaak and our Chancellor, Doctor Adenauer. I should also like to say a special word in memory of another recipient of the Karls Prize who is now dead, the former Italian Premier, Alcide de Gasperi, and recall the warm, human friendship and close co-operation you gentlemen and our Chancellor Adenauer enjoyed with this great European.

In choosing you, President Schuman, to receive the prize, a man has been chosen who is something more to Germans than the great statesman of a neighbouring land and a man of truly European spirit. The choice fell on a real friend, a personal friend of many in this hall today, and a friend and confidant of the German people as a whole. The warmth of your reception, not only in this hall, but in the city of Aachen, and wherever you go throughout Germany, expresses a very profound feeling. You are a popular and respected figure in Germany in a way that hardly any other foreign statesman is.

It all goes back to that historic hour on May 8th 1950 when the

*Speech in Aachen on May 15th 1958 on the presentation of the Karls Prize to Robert Schuman.

French Government of which you were the head announced to the world that it had decided to try to place the relations between the peoples of Europe on a completely new basis whereby each of them would surrender a part of its sovereignty in the interests of all. With this you, your Government and your country opened a new page in history.

Nowhere did the appeal of the French Government meet with more spontaneous approval than in defeated, occupied and dismembered Germany, to which one of the victorious powers now offered the hand of friendship and co-operation. With this a door opened for the first time and we saw a way out of the painful and guilty involvements of the past into a brighter future. The vision that you, President Schuman, opened to us then, a vision which is gradually becoming a reality in the meantime, is the reason for your great popularity in my country.

Let me quote the words which prefaced the declaration of the French Government:

'The peace of the world cannot be preserved without creative efforts of a magnitude in proportion to the danger. The contribution which a vital and organized Europe can make to our civilization is essential for the preservation of peace.'

That was on May 9th 1950. A few weeks later, on June 25th 1950, the Korean war broke out, and once again showed Europe and the whole world the dangers in which we were all living. It does not detract from the greatness of your idea when I say that those dangers encouraged our efforts and quickened our success.

Thanks to your devotion to this idea, and to your conciliatory and yet firm conduct of the negotiations, it was not long before we were able to found the European Coal and Steel Community, which will always be known, at least in Germany, as the Schuman Plan. Whilst you were still French Foreign Minister you had the satisfaction of getting your plan under way, and introducing the new European organizations it required.

In the meantime your European ideas had borne fruit on other fields too. In May 1925 you came to Bonn to sign an agreement with Germany, and shortly afterwards as Foreign Minister you welcomed your European colleagues to Paris for the signing of the European Defence Agreement. It was no fault of yours that this agreement was never implemented, or that not all the ideas we worked out in the constitutional committee for a European political community have come into being.

Set-backs belong as inevitably to politics as they do to the life of the individual. I should begin to fear that there was something wrong with the European idea if it went forward too smoothly without suffering set-backs and disappointments. The ideas embodied in those agreements and proposals have not proved barren. They are still at work in many forms and in many places, thus helping to build the new united Europe we all desire.

When the Messina Conference gave a new impetus to the efforts for European integration you were no longer French Foreign Minister, but in those decisive years you were still active, and, whatever your position, you never ceased to work for the fulfilment of those ideas, whether as a member of the French Government, as a Deputy to the French National Assembly, or as President of the European movement. It was therefore a most excellent decision when on March 19th the inaugural meeting of the joint assembly of European communities elected you its President, so that within eight years from your first plan for a European Coal and Steel Community you were at the head of the first Parliament of Europe.

I do not know whether in May 1950 you could possibly have had any idea of how things would develop, and yet when I look back it seems to me that despite all set-backs and disappointments, our progress was unexpectedly and extraordinarily rapid. We have therefore every reason to look back in gratitude. That you were unanimously elected to your high office by the representatives of all nations will have shown you that your work is appreciated beyond all national and party ties.

In your new role you will be an example and a mentor to us in the future as you were in the past. You were one of the first European statesmen to recognize and to say openly that there can be no future for Europe unless the relationship between France and Germany is placed on a completely new footing. Without the close co-operation and sincere understanding of these two peoples and their governments every attempt to unite Europe will be doomed to failure. This is also the guiding principle of the German Federal Government's policy.

Like you, President Schuman, we do not want to look upon this new Europe as a temporary measure forced upon us by circumstances, as a temporary alliance which will fall to pieces as soon as the outward pressure and the danger which threatens us all is removed.

For us as for you a united Europe is an end in itself. Allow me to repeat your words in September 1953:

'Europe must become a community of nations each one retaining its own way of life but united in joint defence and in constructive achievement. It is not a question of any temporary and provisional solution designed to ward off an exceptional danger or stop a gap in our defence. The problem of Europe does not depend on any communist or Asiatic danger. It is just that this danger makes its solution all the more urgent.'

The first declaration of the French Government on May 9th 1950 was dominated by the idea that Europe must unite for the sake of peace. One year ago another recipient of the Karls Prize, the former Belgian Premier and now Secretary-General of NATO, Paul-Henri Spaak, expressed the same idea in this very hall:

'Beyond all the cruelties of this conflict, beyond all the disruptive passions it aroused, we have gradually realized that this European war which hurled nation against nation was in the last resort nothing but a particularly horrible kind of civil war, because the only defeated power in the Second World War was unquestionably Europe as a whole.'

The European community is intended to serve the cause of peace not only amongst its member States but throughout the world. It is directed against no one and it threatens no one. But in putting an end to the disunity of Europe it also calls a halt to the aggression of a totalitarian system which is fundamentally at variance with us all. Speaking to a well-known Danish journalist in March 1953 you said:

'I am convinced that what was once no more than a splendid dream is now step by step becoming a European reality. But it would be a very dangerous illusion to suppose that everything can be done at one blow. We therefore prefer to do things one at a time, to advance one step at a time in practical matters; and on sober consideration I think we can say that we have made a good start. It is like building a house: brick is laid upon brick until the house is built. Our dream would never have become a reality if we had started straight away to organize the United States of Europe.'

And that is how we propose to go on. Today we can look back with

199

pride and gratitude on what has already been done, but we must not forget that so far we have safeguarded peace, freedom and well-being for part of Europe only. More than half of all Europeans are still living outside the territory in which we have established our European institutions – some of them because for various reasons they have not yet been able to make up their minds to join us; the others because they are prevented against their will from joining us, and this is a particularly sad thought. The name Europe will have its full, proud sound only when all those who feel that they belong with us are able to work together with us in a society based on freedom, peace and security. This, President Schuman, is the great aim to which we pledge ourselves with you.

# 21

## Towards a More Humane World*

TOWARDS a more humane world – that is the theme of our gathering here today. At first it may sound like a commonplace, perhaps even banal, since it is, of course, human beings who have given this world the organization under which we live. The world would therefore be humane in the truest sense of the word if the men who form and shape it were conscious of their moral obligations.

But in truth this theme reveals the whole tragedy of our time. It is a confession that men have failed, that they have not succeeded in shaping that essential sphere, the political, social and economic order, in a way that would permit man to develop fully, free of fear, free of compulsion, and free of peril, limited only by eternal and unchangeable moral law and respect for the rights of his fellow man.

A mere glance at the moral and political state of our age shows with alarming urgency how greatly mankind has failed in this central task, and how far removed we are from the ideal state of a humane world. In one lifetime two world wars have shattered the moral, social, economic and political structure of the world. Societies have arisen over great areas of the world of which one can only say that though they were made by men they were not made for mankind. In such societies man and his personal dignity are not the centre of things, man has been degraded to a mere unit in a rationalized process of production, and belief in the creative power of right has been replaced by worship of the destructive force of might. When they talk of freedom there they mean anarchy, because the moral

*Address to the Academic Festival Session at the World Exhibition in Brussels on August 14th 1958.

obligations of true freedom are denied. And when they dare to talk of tolerance it means only a declaration of moral neutrality. The political expression of this perverse thought is the totalitarian State, which proclaims unrestricted materialism, denies the dignity of man, deprives him of his personality and creates a soulless mass more easy to dominate.

In this state of affairs it is necessary for us to think over what brought it about and how we can oppose it.

In the last resort it came about because mankind was unable to free itself from the individualistic and materialistic outlook of the past century, and in consequence technology, from being the servant of man, became his master. A tremendous technical development involving increasing specialization and automation certainly resulted in a great growth of economic productivity, but man found himself more and more entangled in this technically highly-developed process of production. In consequence his private role and his chance of spiritual development grew narrower and narrower, and he progressively lost touch with spiritual and cultural values, and therefore his true mastery of technology.

In our immediate past it was National Socialism, an inhuman totalitarian system, which showed the world what evil a society of human beings can produce when it deliberately turns its back on all its moral obligations, sets up a mass collective in place of the sum of morally responsible individuals, and replaces belief in justice by propaganda and a glorification of might. Today it is world Communism which threatens the freedom and dignity of man.

Our own lifetime and two world wars have shown the magnitude of the dangers which threaten us, and demonstrated that the destructive urge of a totalitarian system oppresses its own people no less than it menaces the world at large. The dangers are no less now than they were. Unprecedented technological developments have given man such power over natural forces that its proper use in the interests of all mankind would open up splendid prospects for us all. Instead means of destruction have been developed whose exact effects no one quite knows but which seem calculated to destroy the whole of humanity. Truly apocalyptic visions of the future are opening up.

A new factor has now been added to the situation. Many peoples in Asia and Africa seem to have awakened from the sleep of centuries. And they now demand freedom. They want to take their fate into their own hands, but they find themselves saddled with tasks and problems which go beyond their powers. The development they are experiencing is changing the familiar face of the world, and it raises questions for us which we cannot and dare not try to evade.

But it is not enough to analyse the causes of our present disarray no matter how carefully we may go about it. The question we have to answer is: what can be done to make the world a more humane place – not only for ourselves here at home, but all over the world, since men everywhere have the same right as ourselves to live and develop freely. It is not enough to talk of freedom, or even to demand freedom for all men. If we want to be taken seriously we must show unwavering determination to preserve that freedom where it exists, and at the same time to bring it to those men who still lack it – not by force, but by showing them the right use of freedom in our own lives. The fate of millions of our fellow-men now living the lives of modern slaves should constantly remind us of this duty.

The Christian, and the Catholic Christian in particular, is not without resources where such problems are concerned. In the nineteenth century Catholic priests and Catholic laymen came together to formulate the social teachings of the Church. Against materialism, the ultimate expression of unrestricted *laisser-faire*, against the slogans of the class struggle and against class hatred as the expression of early Marxism, they appealed to human dignity, freedom and social justice. There was, of course, nothing fundamentally new in this. The Church has always occupied itself closely with the problems of man's political and social order, and put forward the unchangeable and inalienable basis of its teachings as a guide by which men can live together, as that *lex aeterna* of which Augustine spoke.

These principles of Catholic social teaching are not a ready-made solution for all everyday political questions, and we must not underestimate the specific objective and scientific gravity of the social and economic factors of the day. The Decalogue does not absolve man from his conscientious duty of deciding what is good and what evil. In the same way the acceptance of Catholic social and political principles does not absolve the citizen from his everyday responsibilities. He still has to shape the society in which he lives, and he will do it satisfactorily only if as a thinking, living personality he acts in all Christian responsibility in accordance with those eternally valid principles.

In the nineteenth, and again in our own century, the Church has made two fundamental declarations on the fixed and inalienable limits and aims within whose scope the individual and society, the community and the State, the undertaking and the economy, the nation and the world of nations, can work together in harmony to create those conditions in which man, in which all men, can live according to their higher destiny and to the greater perfection of their personalities. I refer to the two encyclicals *Rerum Novarum* and *Quadragesimo Anno*.

*Rerum Novarum* makes the concept of the commonweal the centre of its observations, and in so doing it determines the right relationship between the individual and society. Individualism and collectivism are equally inhuman: the one because it ignores fellow-man, our neighbour; and the other because it makes the collective absolute in a way that rides rough-shod over the freedom and the dignity of the individual. 'The sphere of the commonweal is human culture,' says Messner; 'that of the individual weal is the human being. They are fundamentally different but fundamentally dependent on each other.' May I remind you that we are not far from the city of Malines here, and it was there that at the beginning of this century a number of courageous and far-sighted men came together to study the application of Christian doctrine to the social problems of their day. The Union des Malines co-operated with the Union de Fribourg to render an enormous service in making known and applying the principles of the encyclical *Rerum Novarum*.

*Quadregesimo Anno* gives us an incomparable formulation of the social and political principle of subsidiary function:

'... just as it is wrong to withdraw from the individual and commit to a group what private enterprise and industry can accomplish, so too it is an injustice, a grave evil and a disturbance of right order, for a larger and higher association to arrogate to itself functions which can be performed efficiently by smaller and lower associations. ... Let those in power, therefore, be convinced that the more faithfully this principle of subsidiary function be followed, and a graded hierarchical order exist between various associations, the greater will be both social authority and social efficiency, and the happier and more prosperous the condition of the common-wealth.'

And we might well add, the more human the State.

204

Indeed, this principle of subsidiary function results in an organic development of State and society because each natural association has its place, its specific tasks and its sphere of activities. In this way not only will the freedom of the individual be safeguarded, but also the free development of those associations which stand between the State and the individual, such as the family, the trade and professional association, the municipality, the region and the county. In this way men are brought together precisely where their cultural, economic and political interests properly lie. On the one hand they will be saved from rootlessness, and on the other hand they will be spared the overriding omnipotence of the State, because natural intermediate organizations will appear of their own right between the individual and the State. A pluralistic conception of justice is the necessary complement to the principle of subsidiary function.

However, this principle of subsidiary function has also its corollary and would allow no association to deal with questions which of their nature can be dealt with satisfactorily only by larger organizations superior in the hierarchy.

This strikes me as of decisive importance for the sphere of international politics, since it allows a clear view over the broad and sometimes chaotic field of international relations. The glorification of the national State and of the principle of absolute sovereignty find their limit in this principle of subsidiary function, and it cannot be ignored without a danger to peace.

'Peace,' says Augustine, 'is concord in orderliness.' The dangerous unrest in our world today is largely due to the fact that the sovereign national State is no longer able to cope with its tasks and its problems on its own, and that it has frequently not yet found the way to international co-operation. The international order capable of preserving peace must therefore be based on the principle of subsidiary function. In other words, the national State must transfer those tasks and that sovereignty which can be shouldered with a greater chance of success by the larger associations. In our present-day society based on a division of labour there are very many such tasks. Consider only the problem of safeguarding peace, controlling disarmament, sharing raw materials, exploring space, extending transport and communications, and co-operating internationally in economic matters.

Just as the principle of subsidiary function extends beyond the sovereign national State, so the commonweal is directed to the good of all mankind. The more earnestly we concern ourselves with this conception of a commonweal the more thoroughly we shall acquaint ourselves with one of the most urgent problems of our time. As long as two-thirds of mankind are underfed we cannot talk conscientiously of a commonweal, and so long must we answer the ceaseless appeal to help those countries less blessed by nature than our own. This is precisely what Pius XII meant when he declared that: 'the welfare of the peoples cannot be properly safeguarded unless it is the common lot of all peoples.' However, one of the conditions of such joint assistance is that the recipient should also contribute to the common good; in other words, that he should subordinate himself to the moral aim of the commonweal as a whole.

Whoever approaches the solution of our political and economic problems armed with these principles need have nothing to fear from these ideologies which are at present on the offensive. Mankind did not have to wait till 1789 before discovering the quality of fraternity; and the 'fraternity' of the modern totalitarian State, which may well suit the life of the termite ant, but has nothing in common with human dignity, will not make the world a happier place to live in. In the spiritual and political confusion of our day Christians can safely fall back on those ideas which represent the wisdom and discernment of the master spirits of the world, and were developed in the light of what we rightly term *lux perpetua*.

I have the great honour to address you as a German and as the representative of the first German Federal Chancellor, Doctor Konrad Adenauer. Together with innumerable others he has attempted to create a new order based on justice and on the eternally valid moral law at least in that part of our Fatherland in which civic freedom and individual responsibility have been re-established. The German people have gone through the lowest depths under a system based on force and the absence of all morality. The overwhelming majority of the German people acknowledge the value and the dignity of man and his individual responsibility. I think I can also speak here for those who recognize the roots of this understanding not directly in Christianity but in the humanism which has developed from it.

That is why Germany is so passionately in favour of European unity, even European unification. Sometimes we may despair and doubt our ability to carry out the task that faces us. But we have not the right to resign ourselves, or to give up. And when we feel our courage sinking then let us recall the inspiring words one of the sternest and most uncompromising critics of these present times, the Frenchman Georges Bernanos, uttered after the last war amidst the ruins of a devastated German town: 'La plus haute forme de l'espérance, c'est le désespoir surmonté.'

# 22

## On the Death of John Foster Dulles*

THE news of the death of the former United States Secretary of State and personal adviser to the President will have caused a deep and sincere feeling of sorrow in the hearts of millions of people in all parts of the world. Both the friends and enemies of John Foster Dulles will agree that with his death an outstanding personality has left the world political stage. His name will always be associated with the eventful and tragic history of our time.

John Foster Dulles brought his own personal style to the guidance of American foreign policy. An unusual profusion of tasks and an unusual burden of responsibility fell to his lot. Enjoying the complete confidence of the President of the United States, whose intimate personal friend he also was, he succeeded in creating an unusually strong position for himself in the political life of our time.

His experience as a brilliant lawyer made him a brilliant negotiator and an outstanding mediator. Filled with an unshakeable belief in the justice of his cause as the representative of the free world, he also had all the qualities which make a great statesman. No one who knew this cool and yet deeply emotional man, stern and yet benevolent, uncompromising and yet understanding, serious and yet serene, could fail to be influenced by his personality. He was a man who recognized no distinction between politics and morality. It was this his friends admired, his opponents respected, and his enemies feared.

Like all great ideas, the conception of American foreign policy as Dulles understood it during the difficult years of his office was fundamentally clear, logical and cogent. Looking back on his life's work this is now apparent even to those who in the confusing ups-

*Obituary in the *Frankfurter Allgemeine Zeitung* on May 25th 1959.

and-downs of everyday politics failed to understand him, and accused him of lacking imagination, and of obstinacy and opportunism.

The tragic and dangerous conflict between East and West under which the whole world suffers was already in existence when he took office. Whoever accused him of not having bridged this antagonism, even of having often stressed it, and sternly called it by its real name, fails to understand the historic significance and the ideological basis of this clash between the free world of the West and the totalitarian and revolutionary system of Communism.

No matter how hard the statesmen responsible may try to find one there is not always a satisfactory answer to all the problems of foreign policy of the day. John Foster Dulles always approached the political facts soberly and seriously. A sense of reality sharpened by long experience saved him from running after the wish-fulfilments some of his critics tried to present as facts. Nevertheless Dulles, far-sighted statesman and understanding human being, was not without hope and confidence.

Despite many disappointments he never lost his conviction that a peaceable relaxation of world political tension was possible, but he knew that this depended on the determination of the Western world to defend its rights under all circumstances. He was never in any doubt about the difficulties ahead, and he was not the man to capitulate to them. He was a statesman determined to surmount them.

The German people on both sides of the Iron Curtain have lost a true and sincere friend in John Foster Dulles, and he always defended their legitimate interests with the passion of the right-thinking man. He regarded it as one of his chief tasks to give Germany the right of self-determination once again. He knew that the unnatural dismemberment of the German people was an expression and a consequence of the world political tension he was anxious to abolish in order to give the whole world peace.

This realization and this intention represented the basis of his close political co-operation with the Federal Government. It was also the basis for the deep and sincere personal friendship which developed between him and Chancellor Doctor Adenauer. From their common thought developed that joint action which has since proved so successful. It will be the aim of German policy to continue this close co-operation with the successor of John Foster Dulles so that the legacy of a good friend may be perpetuated.

Like all great men, John Foster Dulles was an idealist in the best sense of the word. Idealism in thought and realism in action do not exclude, but complement each other. Whoever denies the power of the idea has no alternative but to fall back on might. Whoever refuses to see the facts falls victim to illusions.

How greatly the idea and the reality determined his thought and his action he once at a very critical moment indicated himself when he said that the free world seemed to be more dominated by its differences than by those things on which it was agreed. It decided its foreign policy in full view of the public, and that encouraged its enemies to sow dissension. This was both confusing and exhausting – so much so that now and again one began to feel that everything was useless. But we should always remember that variety was the authentic sign of freedom. The truth was that a dictatorship was never as strong as it looked, whilst a democracy was never as weak as it seemed.

In the political conflicts ahead in the world we shall no longer have the advice and the aid of John Foster Dulles, but should we ever feel doubt and discouragement let us remember his work and the profound confidence that inspired it.

# 23

## Stresemann the European*

Two years have passed since as Minister for Foreign Affairs I first had official occasion to speak of the memory of the former Chancellor and Foreign Minister, Gustav Stresemann. That was on May 9th 1958 on the eve of what would have been the eightieth birthday of that great German patriot and statesman. In admiration and gratitude the Foreign Office remembered the man who for long years had been at its head, and in the name of my collaborators I pledged myself to continue in the same spirit the work he had begun, and to persist with the same determination that had guided his own actions. On that day I unveiled a tablet in the Foreign Office as a permanent memorial to him and a symbol for our future activity.

We are now celebrating the thirty-fifth anniversary of a day that will always be associated with Gustav Stresemann's political activities. Thirty-five years ago today Gustav Stresemann, Aristide Briand and Sir Austen Chamberlain signed an agreement in the little town of Locarno. It went into history under the name of the Locarno Pact as one of the most important political decisions of the period between the two world wars.

I consider it as a particular honour to be here today as the representative of the Federal Government and the successor of Gustav Stresemann to unveil this memorial. Two other tablets which are to be unveiled at the same time are in memory of those two other statesmen who brought about the Locarno Pact with him: Aristide Briand and Sir Austen Chamberlain.

It would lead too far if I were to try to deal with all the errors and confusion that preceded the Locarno Pact. The First World War

*Memorial address delivered on October 16th 1960.

211

belonged to the past, and peace treaties were the order of the day, but the tension and the conflict brought about between the nations by four years of bitter warfare had not been resolved. Inner political struggles accompanied by inflation and near civil war conditions had brought Germany to the verge of chaos. But the foreign policy of the young Weimar Republic seemed to be taking a dangerous path too. The Ruhr conflict, the occupation of the Rhineland, and the reparations negotiations poisoned the international atmosphere to an alarming extent and threatened to condemn any serious and courageous initiative to failure.

The impression created by the signing of the Locarno Pact was therefore all the more striking. Three men met who were conscious not only of their responsibilities to their own countries but to history. I shall not be denigrating the achievement of this great German statesman when I say that although he was a man of independent mind, many-sided experience, wide knowledge and great determination, the successes he met with as a statesman were to a great extent due to the fact that he had to do with congenial men who understood him and whom he understood – with Briand, the classic example of a brilliant French parliamentarian drawing his strength from the great traditions of his country's civilization, and with Sir Austen Chamberlain, whose studied reserve did not conceal his objectivity, his determination and his great humanity.

I do not propose in this short address to concern myself with the details of the Locarno Pact. Let it suffice for me to quote the observations of Aristide Briand on the signing of the Pact in London:

'Unless we regard this agreement as a draft constitution for the whole European family of nations it will have been an empty gesture that will lead to much disappointment. For centuries our peoples have faced each other on the battlefield, shedding their blood and sacrificing the flower of their youth. The Locarno Pact will achieve its object if such blood-letting never occurs again, if our wives and mothers never have to mourn again, if our towns and villages are never again devastated, if our young men are never again mutilated. Our peoples faced each other with equal heroism on the battlefield; let them now face each other on the no less glorious field of peaceful competition.'

When we recall these words we realize the full tragedy of the development from the Locarno Pact to the Second World War, the collapse of the Third Reich and all the terrible catastrophes which came upon the world and whose consequences we have not yet overcome. After the signing of the pact Stresemann declared:

'We have undertaken this responsibility because we are convinced that only the peaceable co-existence of States and nations can safeguard that development which is more important for Europe than any other part of the world because its peoples have suffered so much in the years now behind us.'

Despite all opposition it began to look as though he were right, and a few years later Briand electrified the world when at the League of Nations Assembly he first talked about 'the United States of Europe'. And when a journalist asked him whether he had already begun the work to realize this plan and whether he had any hopes of success, he replied with superb confidence: 'There is no need to begin the work; it has already begun.'

Today we ask ourselves how it came about that this splendid conception failed, how it came about that such daring realism went unrewarded. For an answer we must go back to those days and recall the opposition these statesmen had to contend with in their own countries and beyond their own frontiers. It seemed an impossible task for Briand to persuade his countrymen to clear their minds of the psychological consequences of the world war, to overcome the historical prejudices against an understanding with Germany, and to realize that France's true security must lie not in the clauses of a dictated peace, but in agreements freely arrived at with Germany as an equal partner and member of the community of nations. It took all the extraordinary ability, eloquence and energy of this altogether exceptional man to achieve such an aim.

How much more difficult was the furrow Stresemann had to plough! For years he literally fought for the soul of the German people, and nothing was spared him in the struggle. A wave of hatred, bitter slander and base enmity poured over him. When he needed a free hand to carry out his far-sighted plans abroad he had to wear himself out in domestic struggles at home. Men who had forgotten everything and learned nothing libelled and slandered him, and the German Reichstag witnessed a scene hardly paralleled in its baseness. He made his last speech to the League of Nations Assembly on September 9th 1929, having had to postpone it twice on account of

213

heart attacks; and when he finally delivered it he was already a dying man:

'I believe that the wide field of man's fight for the conquest of nature offers sufficient possibilities for heroism and for devoting our lives to great ideas. Here is an enormous field on which man's relation to the cosmos can be studied and perhaps brought nearer a solution for the benefit of all. Our present task is the more sober one of bringing the peoples closer to each other and resolving their differences. They are not yet as near to each other as we would like to see them. There are still conflicts. There is hard work ahead to reduce these differences and bring us nearer to what we all desire. Cheers and enthusiasm alone will not do it.'

The man who said that then returned to Berlin where he found that people like von Hugenberg and Hitler were demanding a People's Referendum to impose severe punishments on 'traitors' such as himself. His answer was

'To threaten men with a charge of treason when they are working with all their might, and to the detriment of their health, for freedom is an infamy which not even the sharpest political struggle can excuse. Those who have organized this referendum are irresponsibly exploiting the sacred national feelings of the German people and their present economic adversity.'

A few days later Gustav Stresemann died. Then the seed sown by the demagogues, the fanatics and the criminals produced a great harvest. Hitler and his followers came to power. They destroyed the monument which had been erected here in Mainz to the memory of Stresemann, and they sought to efface his historical achievement from the minds of the German people. Those who had slandered him and persecuted him with hatred to the day of his death now led the German people into the greatest catastrophe in their whole history.

Allow me to express my sincere thanks to those who have restored the Stresemann memorial. It posthumously honours a great German statesman, a man who had shaken off the chains of the past and courageously formed a picture of the future, which, despite all difficulties, seemed near to fulfilment even then. What would the German people and the whole world have been spared if the ideas so courageously embodied in the Locarno Pact had become a reality!

It gives me particular pleasure and satisfaction to welcome Frau

Käthe Stresemann and one of her sons here, and I can assure them that we feel ourselves profoundly at one with that great German statesman, Gustav Stresemann. In honouring his memory today we are also pledging ourselves to his political ideas, and we are determined to go forward along the path he laid down.

The great work of European unification is not yet completed, but I feel that we have already laid a sound basis on which we can continue to build. The realization of this great idea must not fail a second time although in the meantime perhaps our task has grown even more difficult. We are engaged in a hard and unrelenting struggle which we cannot evade, because today two mutually exclusive ideas of the world confront each other. The maintenance and increase of individual well-being, and the safeguarding of national independence and national character are high aims which we neither deny nor intend to abandon, but we shall attain them only if we place human freedom above all else.

Freedom is in danger today. We shall be able to preserve it only if the free peoples of the world abandon many cherished but outworn traditions and close their ranks. In working for this we are carrying out the legacy of the man whose memory we are gathered here to honour. It is late in the day, but perhaps not too late.

# 24

# Obedience, Freedom and Conscience*

It is not easy to interpret and understand what happened on July 20th 1944. On July 20th 1954 I was in Berlin when Federal President Heuss declared that nothing should move us more than the opportunity of declaring ourselves on this day and expressing our gratitude.

Perhaps those of us who experienced and survived that day, what went before and what came after, should remain silent, for we witnessed the inner conflict between duty and conscience, between obedience and honour, which drove the men to revolt, whose memory we hold in deep respect today. I shall not even attempt to deal with the conflict of feelings which tormented and spiritually rent the men and women of those days. A Government which pretended to speak in the name of the German people had plunged us into terrible crime and the world into unspeakable misfortune. Nevertheless it demanded blind obedience from all Germans. But to obey meant to become an accomplice in crime and murder. To refuse obedience could mean to condemn the German people to destruction, for the whole world had come together to punish the German people for the injustice and the crimes which had been comitted in their name. And amongst those who demanded this punishment were some who had neither the moral right nor the political mission to impose it.

This is what moves and stirs us so deeply. The confrontation was not clearly between justice and injustice, between slavery and freedom. The fateful entanglement into which the German people had been led, and the truly diabolical alternatives with which they were

*Speech delivered on July 20th 1961 on the seventeenth anniversary of the attempt to overthrow Hitler.

216

faced, raises the conflict in which these men suffered from the plane of the political into that of moral responsibility.

We know that the men whose memory we are honouring today did not seek to evade the question. Thank God what they thought, what they said and what they planned has been preserved. I will not try to express in my own inadequate words what moved them. Let them speak for themselves.

After his arrest one of them, Father Delp, wrote:

'In these weeks of constraint I have realized that human beings are always lost, are always victims of their environment, their circumstances and the pressures exercised on them unless they are capable of great inner breadth and freedom. Whoever is not at home in an atmosphere of freedom, which remains inviolable and inalienable in defiance of all outward forces and circumstances, is lost. The hour in which human freedom is born is the hour in which we confront God.'

He expressed what the others thought, even those he did not know and who did not know him. That is the real secret of July 20th: that men who were acting with different political aims, from different political pasts and from different social backgrounds, acknowledged a joint task and a joint responsibility. They did it without knowing each other, and they continued to do it when they did know each other.

One of those whose name is on the tablet I am here to unveil, Adam von Trott zu Solz, wrote on the day he was condemned to death:

'It was an attempt deriving from the consciousness of our country's power to defend and maintain her right, unchangeable in all modern transformations and difficulties, and her profound and indispensable contribution, against the encroachments of powers and ideas foreign to her nature.'

That was what they all thought when they came together, first driven silently by inner compulsion and the restlessness of conscience. And so together they decided to raise up again that justice that had been trodden underfoot in Germany, and to establish it again in all spheres of human relations. The fear of God instead of violence and terrorism; truth and decency in place of lies and selfishness, because the life of a whole people, just as the life of an individual, requires absolutely valid standards just as it requires justification before God

217

And what they wanted we also know now. In their appeal to the German people there is a passage I should like to quote:

> 'We should be unworthy of our fathers and deserve the contempt of our children if we had not enough courage to do everything, absolutely everything, to ward off the terrible danger that threatens us and win back our self-respect.'

Men came together from all classes of the German people and from all spheres of its public life to turn their beliefs into action on July 20th 1944. They followed those who had acted before them, and they gave an example to those who sacrificed life and freedom after them to free the survivors and spare them entanglement in the handiwork of murder.

The names of many members of the Foreign Office are inscribed on this memorial tablet. I am proud to honour them today and I bow my head to their memory and to their relatives who are still with us.

Let me read the names inscribed here:

Albrecht Graf von Bernstorff

Eduard Brücklmeier

Herbert Gollnow

Hans-Berend von Haeften

Ulrich von Hassell

Otto Kiep

Richard Kuenzer

Hans Litter

Herbert Mumm von Schwarzenstein

Friedrich-Werner Graf von der Schulenburg

Adam von Trott zu Solz

Let no one pass this tablet without heed. The memory of these men must be kept alive, particularly in the hearts of the younger members of the Foreign Office. These young men have been spared the conscious knowledge and the responsibility for the period of the Third Reich. They were not placed before this tragic conflict between duty and conscience.

Let the joint determined will of the whole German people spare us any repetition of such a thing. Those of you who are growing into responsibility have an obligation of watchfulness. You will fulfil your duty if you always remain conscious that obedience and freedom find their limits in the moral obligations of the individual before his own conscience. And what is conscience but the voice of God in man?

The man without conscience is not obedient but merely subservient. He is not free but merely unbridled. If we recognize these standards we shall uphold the legacy of those men who gave their lives for the freedom and honour of the German people.

# 25

# On the Nine-hundredth Anniversary of the Consecration of Speyer Cathedral*

THERE are few monuments on German soil which so clearly indicate the close relationship of the Germans with Western history, and their own inner strength and unity, as Speyer Cathedral. Today we celebrate the nine-hundredth anniversary of the consecration of this magnificent building, perhaps the most impressive on German soil, and in doing so we cannot avoid the urgent question as to whether the power and confidence it represents still exist in our own day. Are we still conscious of this unity, and have we still the strength and the will to let our actions be determined by this consciousness?

Our situation today is the result of innumerable outside influences. They were unavoidable, like the social, technological, industrial and scientific revolution we have witnessed and are still witnessing. But was it unavoidable that we should have accepted the alleged independent momentum of this development, and that we should apparently still do so? Was it inevitable that man should capitulate to this development and allow himself to be forced more and more from the responsible position of an active subject to that of a passive object?

The situation in which we now find ourselves derives its character from the fact that the past few hundred years have seen the dissolution of traditional standards of belief and forms of thought, and, indeed, of man's whole way of life. The principle that the State and not the individual is the proper vessel of man's political order has increasingly established itself, until today it is widely accepted that public order is the proper determining factor in man's existence.

We know, of course, that the life of the individual does depend

*Address delivered on September 10th 1961.

220

elementarily on the life of the community to which he belongs and on the relationship between that community and others, but we do not believe that this necessarily must be so in principle. We do not believe that man is essentially determined by the political community he belongs to.

It is a remarkable thing that the relativity of values seems to falter at this principle – indeed, even seems inclined to recognize it as the only still absolute principle. This process is reflected in the structure of the State by the increasing tendency to centralism and bureaucracy. It began in the days of Absolutism, it continued with the French Revolution, and it grows without limit in the totalitarianism of our own day. It leads to the de-humanizing of man, and to the de-personalization of the individual. It ends in the all-powerful machine in which the individual is a mere cog that can be replaced at any time should it be thought to function inadequately.

Parallel with this development, which characterizes a new historical epoch, we have seen the rise of modern means of mass destruction. They are nothing less than a tool created by man by means of which humanity can biologically utterly destroy itself.

And so we are faced with a double question: first of all a question relating to the unity of our history and thus the preservation of our Christian Western heritage despite all changes against the destructive forces of totalitarianism. And secondly the question of what we can do to ward off the threatening possibility of the end of history altogether. And the history of mankind can end in two ways: by the politico-spiritual destruction of all human values under totalitarian pressure, and by the physical destruction of mankind. The possible end of human history is brought dramatically nearer by the fact that where it exists the totalitarian system threatens the physical destruction of mankind in order to bring the world into its power. And there are people who are prepared to capitulate before the apparent insolubility of the problem, who seem to be prepared to accept the spiritual destruction of mankind in the hope of escaping its physical destruction. It is reminiscent of the man who commits suicide for fear of death.

But there is a way in which we can offer vigorous resistance, and that is to fall back on values which are absolute and eternally unchangeable. We must take our stand on what the recent encyclical *Mater et Magister* says for all Christians, whether Catholic or Protestant:

'The individual is the basis, the aim and the vessel of all those institutions in which social life finds its expression and its realization – individual human beings as they are and as they should be.'

This cathedral, the anniversary of whose founding we are now celebrating, is, it seems to me, an expression of such thought. Its artistically ordered lines reflect the spiritual attitude of the time in which it was built and of the men who built it.

At the same time it is an expression of pride in planning and humility in dedication. It is still a monument to the vigorous confidence and splendid pride of those emperors and the pious trust that imbued its builders.

In it we recognize the significance of the fruitful polarity – not without its dangers – which alone gives birth to all great human achievements; a polarity which becomes fruitful when pride and humility, self-confidence and belief form a true synthesis. This polarity becomes dangerous when hubris replaces pride and servility replaces humility in an insoluble antithesis.

As this cathedral was erected so must man's political society be erected. The memory of a great past is both a task and an obligation. The great plan that was carried into execution nine hundred years ago is a tremendous appeal to our own self-confidence. This vast pile was erected by those emperors to the glory of God, and it reminds us that pride and self-confidence are reconcilable with pious dedication.

That is the lesson of this edifice, and if we are prepared to learn it then we are not at the end of human history. We shall then be capable of watchfully, courageously and successfully warding off the danger of spiritual and physical destruction that threatens us.

# Resignation Statement*

THE seriousness of the situation of our foreign policy demands the immediate formation of a politically effective Federal Government able to take part in the discussions of our allies and co-operate with them in their decisions. For this the basic policy of such a government must be approved by the German Bundestag.

A public discussion about the person of the Foreign Minister at such a moment would be intolerable. It would also be dangerous and bad for the prestige of the Federal Republic in the eyes of the world, because the cause is at stake and not the person. Behind the demand for a change in the person is in reality a demand for a change in policy.

A Cabinet Minister, and in particular the Foreign Minister, needs the confidence of the head of government responsible for the general lines of government policy if he is to work effectively. But he also needs the confidence of those parliamentary forces on which the government is based. The unusual demand that the Foreign Minister should have another Cabinet Minister at his side suggests that the probable coalition partner lacks that confidence. Apart from a say in the formation of foreign policy by the Cabinet the Free Democratic Party also demands a direct say in the work of the Foreign Office.

Such an arrangement cannot be reconciled with the constitutional responsibility of a Federal Minister, who is responsible to the Bundestag as a whole, and not to any individual section of it.

Public opinion might be led to feel, wrongly, that the obstacle to the formation of a new government was the demand of the present Foreign Minister that he should be a member of any future Cabinet. This mistaken idea must be rebutted.

*October 31st 1961.

On Saturday, October 28th 1961, I therefore wrote to the Federal Chancellor with the request that he should propose the acceptance of my resignation by the Federal President as soon as possible. At the same time I informed the Chairman of the German Christian Democratic Union, and the Chairman of the parliamentary association of the Christian Democratic Union and the Christian Social Union that I had decided against becoming a member of the new Federal Government.